A BRIEF HIST

Mike Moore held the portfolios of Overseas Trade and Marketing, Tourism, Recreation and Sport in New Zealand's Fourth Labour Government from 1984–90. Later he became Minister of Foreign Affairs and External Relations and a deputy Finance Minister. He served briefly as Prime Minister before the 1990 General Election. He became a member of the Eminent Persons on Trade Group in 1989.

Also by Mike Moore:

On Balance
Beyond Today
The Added Value Economy
The Pacific Parliament
Hard Labour
Fighting for New Zealand
Children of the Poor

On *Fighting for New Zealand* (1993)

... a courageous effort to get New Zealanders to rethink the assumptions that have underpinned public policies and popular expectations for decades, and to make fundamental changes so that New Zealand can hold its own and thrive in the economy of the 21st century.

–Lee Hsien Loong
Deputy Prime Minister
Singapore

... a thoughtful and incisive analysis, not only of New Zealand's national development dilemmas, but also of the great challenges all nations face in today's drastically changed international setting.

– Ali Alatas
Minister for Foreign Affairs
Indonesia

Mike Moore has tackled the hardest task – regenerating the thinking of a political party. This is not just of interest in Australasia, but around the world where people are seeking an alternative to unrelenting and harsh market forces.

– Bob Carr MP
Leader of the Opposition
New South Wales, Australia.

On *Children of the Poor* (1996)

Hard-hitting and provocative, Children of the Poor *is designed to galvanise a nation into action. Violence, gang activities, drug usage, mental health, liquor laws, teenage suicides, truancy, pregnancy in unmarried teenages – all these issues, and others, are dealt with by the author in the only way he knows how – straight from the shoulder.*

– Jack Ross

A BRIEF HISTORY
OF THE
FUTURE

Citizenship of the Millennium

Mike Moore

SHOAL BAY PRESS

First published in 1998 by
Shoal Bay Press Ltd
Box 17-661, Christchurch

Reprinted 2001

Cartoon on p.5 by Tom Scott

ISBN 0 908704 77 1

Printed by Rainbow Print Ltd, Christchurch

DEDICATION

This book is dedicated to the elected and appointed public servants who year after year seek negotiated settlements to our differences. These people are the unknown soldiers whose work has made a difference in our search for peace, progress and security.

CONTENTS

GLOSSARY OF ABBREVIATIONS

ACT	Formerly Association of Consumers and Taxpayers, a New Zealand political party
ANC	African National Congress
ANZAC	Australia-New Zealand Army Corps: joint WWI military force; now a generic term describing Aust/New Zealand co-operation and traditions
APEC	Asia-Pacific Economic Co-operation forum
ASEAN	Association of South East Asian Nations
CAP	Common Agriculture Policy
CDR	Closer Defence Relations between New Zealand and Australia
CER	Closer Economic Relations between New Zealand and Australia
COMECON	The communist bloc economic and trade regulation system during the Cold War years
DPRK	Democratic People's Republic of Korea
EU	European Union
FAO	Food and Agriculture Organisation (US)
GATT	General Agreement on Tariffs and Trade
GDP	Gross Domestic Product
GNP	Gross National Product
KPMG	An international accounting and professional services company
ICFTU	International Confederation of Free Trade Unions
ILO	International Labour Organisation
IMF	International Monetary Fund
IRA	Irish Republican Army
IT	Information technology
MAI	Multilateral Agreement on Investment
MEA	Multilateral Environment Agreement
MERCOSUR	A South American free-trade framework agreement
MMP	Mixed Member Proportional electoral system
NAFTA	North American Free Trade Agreement
NATO	North Atlantic Treaty Organisation
NGO	Non-governmental organisation
OE	Overseas experience (colloquial)
OECD	Organisation for Economic Co-operation and Development
SPARTECA	South Pacific Regional Trade and Economic Co-operation Agreement
UN	United Nations
UNHCR	United Nations High Commission for Refugees
UNICEF	United Nations Children's Fund
USTR	United States Trade Representative (Cabinet Minister equivalent)
WTO	World Trade Organisation

Acknowledgments and Preface

I BEGAN THIS BOOK formally 18 months ago. All books, of course, reflect a lifetime of experiences, books, papers, meetings and opinions that have helped mould one's own views. My objective in writing this book was to clarify my own thinking in a complex area, and also to answer the critics of more open and integrated economies.

A decade ago I saw myself as a patriot in my campaign for freer trade and a more open global economy. I was fighting for jobs in my country and helping to build a safer, more integrated, prosperous world.

Yet people like me who advance these ideals have found ourselves caught in a backlash. We are seen by some to be selling out our country and even accused of trying to abolish the nation state. The opposite is the truth. We see ourselves as advancing the integrity and sovereignty of the nation state by protecting and promoting independence through interdependence.

I'm an optimist: I think the next century could be wonderful. We have a splendid opportunity to help ourselves and help others by international co-operation. Over one and a half billion people's living standards have doubled in the past decade and a half.[1]

However, it is clear that the powerful elite of business people, politicians and intellectuals are out of touch with the general population, the people who can see the pain of these policies but not the gain. The elite throughout the world have more in common with each other than with their constituents and shareholders. This is not new; it was also true of the princes and merchants of earlier times.

In 1996, when for a while it looked as if Labour might form a government, I met with the Secretary of the Foreign Affairs and Trade Department and told him that if we were government we would have to establish a new embassy. 'Where?' he groaned. 'Wellington,' I replied. 'We no longer just have to convince reluctant Americans or Europeans. We now have to convince bruised New Zealanders.'

This book in part is an attempt to overcome this democratic deficit. There is a deficit in understanding, because no one is leading, or explaining why.

Let's not idealise international trade. It doesn't provide a redistribution mechanism for wealth or provide a health or education system; nor can it provide proper

9

environmental regimes, which are both a domestic and an international imperative. But it can provide the security and economic growth necessary for enduring
solutions to be reached.

International rules can be complementary to domestic rules because domestic
solutions on their own will not succeed in the new borderless world.

Writing this book gave me an opportunity to study Treaty of Waitangi issues
from an historical global perspective. The rights of indigenous people are high
on the international agenda. New Zealand is not alone. How we manage and lead
to restore justice and confront these historical demons will shape the future of
our nation. I suggest we try something radical. Let's try democracy: we've tried
everything else.

This book is about how we move from a century of coercion to a new century
of persuasion. It is not a book for specialists. I admire and respect specialists. But
the years I have spent in politics have convinced me that our collective ability to
understand, with ever-increasing precision, the minutiae of any given topic comes
with a price attached. That price is the crowding out of the generalist and those
who see the bigger picture. I would go further: there is almost a fear of attempting
a grand synthesis. The fear of ridicule – in this case by holders of specialist knowledge – is a powerful disincentive to those who would, by inclination, wish to
bring disparate ideas together.

I accept this but choose to ignore it. This book is indeed primarily a synthesis.
Readers will see I have borrowed extensively from thinkers of all shades of political opinion. I have chosen to quote liberally from them because I feel they have
something valuable to say. My target audience is a broad one. My purpose is 'political' – in what I hope is the finest sense of that much-maligned word: to try to
define the issues all political systems have to grapple with in the age of globalisation.

There are many I must thank for their assistance in this book's preparation.
Some don't even know they were of assistance, but often just talking about issues
helped. Special mention must be made of the New Zealand Parliamentary Li-
brary, those anonymous folk on the Internet, many non-governmental organisations (NGOs), the various embassies based in Wellington, colleagues from many
parties and Parliaments, the dedicated people in the New Zealand public service
and the researchers whose work I lifted from all the great international agencies.
Above all, I thank God that I live in such interesting times, where such information and opportunity abound.

Mike Moore
August 1998

Introduction

NO NATION, ANY MORE than any individual, can hope to prosper isolated and cut off from others. History has proven that New Zealand's isolation has never been a defence from the drama of international events. Just as the world's economy has globalised so have its problems and solutions. From whaling to child labour to terrorism, no nation can hope to achieve peace and progress alone. It's of no use if one nation cleans up the air or water within its own territory but its neighbours do not. Aids cannot be cured or contained by any individual nation's actions. These days, no single economy can even run a tax system without the co-operation of others.

The challenges of security, stability, economic growth, the fight against organised crime, and for human rights all need international solutions. No nation, grand or small, can ever hope to assist with or be the beneficiary of the solution of the great issues of our age without the co-operation of others. We are all in the same boat whether we like it or not.

The competitive advantage our species enjoys over other species is our ability to learn, enjoy, adapt and improve ideas from other cultures. We have progressed because of this cross-cultural pollination. History shows that closed, chauvinistic cultures and societies perish, while open economies and societies flourish.

Protectionism in all its forms retards progress by suffocating change and slowing down our ability to learn, adapt and improve. You can't avoid change by closing your eyes to it. Pulling the blanket over your head will not make the bogeyman go away. Of course sweet dreams and fairytales are easier to sell to anxious voters. But assuming the economic and social foetal position, hoping the world will go away, is not a valid option.

In New Zealand the old unions, breweries and religious wowsers combined in a fatal coalition to insist we couldn't have licensed restaurants, and had to close our pubs by 6 o'clock. Who would want to return to those bad old days?

Even the humble spud was opposed by the merchants and church in its day. A church leader railed against the potato as being a dangerous narcotic, almost as bad as tea. The merchants and farmers wanted to protect their profits and market control against this dangerous, competitive new crop. What if the people actually wanted them? A campaign was duly launched. And their direct intellectual descendants are still at it: these days they oppose cheap cars being imported.

The actions of these self-serving protectionists might seem ludicrous today, but as Machiavelli said: 'The Reformer has for enemies all those who do well out of present conditions and for lukewarm supporters those who might do well out of the new conditions.' Fear and self-interest are great motivators.

There's no going back on the changes that are upon us. There never is. One hundred years ago 80 per cent of New Zealand's jobs were on the land. Now we produce more meat, wool and timber, but fewer than 10 per cent of our jobs are based on these resources. Britain produces more coal with 20,000 workers than it did with 500,000 three generations ago.

Alvin Toffler, the profound and prolific American futurist, wrote of the three great waves of changes in world history. The first, the agricultural revolution, took thousands of years to play itself out. The second wave, the industrial revolution, took a mere 300 years. The third wave, the information age, will take just a few decades. The pace of change is accelerating. Toffler coined the phrase 'future shock', also the title of his bestselling book, to describe the effects of this acceleration of change.

All such profound and historic change is accompanied by violence and distrust as the agony of the loss of the past blacks out the promise of the future. In the face of such pain there are two choices.

Said Toffler, in his book *Creating a New Civilization*:

> What is needed is a clear distinction between rearguard politicians who wish to preserve or restore an unworkable past and those who are ready to make a transition to what we call a Third Wave information society. If nothing else, global competition means we cannot go back to the conformity, uniformity, bureaucracy and brute force economy of the assembly line.

Only one choice, really.

It's a bit like Iraq facing the information-age military response of the US in the Gulf War. Saddam Hussein's industrial-age military machine did not stand a chance. Or the massacre of the Mahdi insurrection by Anglo-Egyptian forces in 1898: an agricultural-age army was destroyed by an industrial-age force.

An equal threat to the powerful and the vested interests is a new form of democratic and popular response to the issues of the day. The new information age means that electronic-based grassroots pressure groups and the media have more power than most politicians. A prime ministerial press conference takes more detailed planning and is taken more seriously these days than Question Time in Parliament. An interview with Paul Holmes is worth more to a politician than publishing a book. Winning a few minutes' affectionate attention from Linda Clark, TVNZ's senior political reporter, is more politically rewarding than visiting Hamilton every month to meet voters in person.

The information age means that communications will never be the same. It's a talkback, telecratic democracy. How we learn, what we eat, our values, our vote and our ethics are more and more influenced by forces outside our homes, our workplaces, even our country. History, as always, is a great teacher, and it is by examining history that we will gain clues as to the way to handle the future.

What is it about our species that has driven us to this point? How did the nation state develop? How did we evolve from civilisations in which kings were seen to have a God-given mandate to a more egalitarian, humanist age?

In early nation-to-nation dealings, did trade follow the flag, or vice versa? Did commercial and political international law follow the merchant ships and battleships, or vice versa? Why is it that some tribes, nations and civilisations prosper and others don't? Did economic freedoms create or follow political freedoms? What does globalisation mean? Is it a danger to sovereignty, or the guarantor of it?

As we look back we will see that all these great historic waves of change have one thing in common: all been accompanied by violent resistance, unemployment and great distrust and hatred of leaders. The fact that change is inevitable has never stopped us blaming its agents.

Just as the invention of steam and then its application to rail and ships changed the power structures of the world, the new highways of the future – the information highways – are changing the way we talk to each other and do business. How does a progressive government prepare for this, and advance the interests of its people while protecting its most vulnerable citizens in such a time of historic readjustment?

In today's economy neither the traditional Keynesian nor monetarist remedies work well. To cope with the Great Depression, John Maynard Keynes, we recall, urged deficit spending by government to put money into consumers' pockets. Once consumers had the money, they would rush out and buy things. This in turn would lead manufacturers to expand their plants and hire more workers. Goodbye unemployment. Monetarists urged manipulation of interest rates or money supply instead, to increase or decrease purchasing power as needed.

These days, pumping money into the consumer's pocket may simply send it flowing overseas without doing anything to help the domestic economy. An American buying a new TV set or compact disc player merely sends dollars to Japan, South Korea, Malaysia or elsewhere. That purchase doesn't add jobs at home to the same extent.

A new solution is required. That solution lies in economic internationalism, based on rules decided upon by sovereign governments. This idea is not so very radical. It simply builds on the ideals and institutions developed at Bretton Woods, first advanced by Woodrow Wilson and given practical meaning by Franklin D. Roosevelt.

Democracy and access to education liberate the skills and genius of all people regardless of race and gender. Equality is good economics. If a nation's freedom can be measured by its level of democracy, surely this truth must be capable of extension to the realm of international dealings.

Totalitarian societies always go backwards because they are not open to the freedom of ideas, commerce and information (or even humour – there are few joke books about Stalin, Hitler or Mao, but everyone knows the melancholy humour of Abraham Lincoln and inspirational wit of Winston Churchill).

This book argues for openness and the rule of international law. It invites us as citizens of the new millennium to build respect and trust in international institutions and the rule of law as a civilised arena in which we can conduct our affairs, resolve our differences and promote progress to ensure our economic, political and environmental security.

Internationalism is not new. Like nationalism it has been promoted by villains and saints alike. At the core of all the great religions is a proposition that there is a common humanity and common rights – so long as we accept their god. The Marxist ideal of a universal proletariat united by class coming together and the liberal dream of a big melting pot were also illusions. Archaeologists keep discovering ruins and monuments built to celebrate individuals and empires whose power was thought to be immortal. There will always be change: democracy encourages it to happen peacefully. People are citizens, not subjects. But true individual liberty is impossible unless people have access to opportunity, and the key to that door is skill and education. Tyrants always try to keep that door closed. Their power cannot withstand the scrutiny that freedom of expression and choice demands.

For the last 50 years international politics has been dominated by the Cold War, which intellectually corrupted and distorted our vision and global institutions. It was a vital war to win, and it was won. Or, rather, Marxism failed. The Cold War perverted the decolonisation process throughout the world as emerging countries were courted, their economies, politics and cultures transformed into surrogate battlegrounds. These days we are returning to more ancient rivalries between cultures.

The clashes of the future will not be so much ideological as cultural and economic. While the world is regionalising and globalising, smaller and frequently ancient political units are seeking recognition. For the first time in 300 years Scotland is to have its own Parliament. A party promoting an independent state for northern Italy is in coalition government. Czechoslovakia is now two nations, the Czech and Slovak republics. Yet the European Union and NATO are expanding, with both new republics seeking membership.

The demand for recognition by the Kurds, the Scots, and by indigenous people from Canada, the United States, Australia and New Zealand is part of a profound historical movement. At first glance these twin movements of globalisation and localisation, even tribalism, look like a clash of contradictions. Not so: they are opposite sides of the same coin. As people experience globalisation, they will want more and more to assert their individuality, independence and cultures. That's a good thing: nobody wants just one world football team.

The principle of subsidiarity holds that decision-making power should be devolved to the lowest level of power consistent with the nature of the problem. Thus, in today's world, since certain problems or issues have to be addressed at the supra-national level (e.g. cross-border pollution) the nation state is too small to take all the decisions in this area. In short, the principle holds that the decision-making process moves up in scale. But equally, according to the principle of subsidiarity, many decisions formerly taken at the nation state level should be delegated to small aggregates of power, e.g. the local government level. The nation state again has to cede power, but this time downwards, not upwards.

This trend poses complex issues for policymakers. In the United Nations and elsewhere worthy souls are working to thrash out issues of self-determination and sovereignty vis a vis the role of the nation state. It is in such international forums that our hope for the future lies because what is happening is not confined to one particular part of the world.

This book advances the doctrine of independence through interdependence. It argues that the interests and independence of sovereign states are safeguarded and promoted through international agreements, treaties and institutions. The true patriot, the true nationalist, must now be an internationalist. For countries like New Zealand, it means gaining leverage through engagement. It allows us to box above our weight division. We need to create and strengthen common institutions because they in turn create common values, goals, objectives and eventually common policies and collective achievements.

The nation state is the basic unit in global matters, just as the family is the basic unit in domestic policy considerations. No family or nation has the right to disturb or violate its neighbours. Each nation's prosperity and well-being is based on the affluence and purchasing power of its neighbours and trading partners. Engagement with and agreement between nations will in the end get us closer to solutions. What will no longer work, even by the greatest power, is unilateral action, whether that unilateral action be economic or even military.

In economic terms I see the globe as a series of circles within a great overarching circle. Smaller circles representing CER, NAFTA, APEC, EU and MERCOSUR are all surrounded by the larger circle of the WTO. Some of these regional trading arrangements currently fit more easily than others with the principles of the multilateral trading system. But nothing is fixed. New Zealand and Australia's first attempt in 1965 to integrate their economies in a free trade agreement (curiously also called NAFTA) would hardly bear close scrutiny today, so wide were its departures from certain underlying principles of the multilateral system. CER radically addressed these shortcomings, but it would never have occurred without that first, albeit imperfect, experiment with regionalism.

On a much larger scale, even the Common Agricultural Policy of the former EC was adjusted to the realities of the multilateral trading system in the course of the Uruguay Round.

In short, I am convinced that the dynamic of globalisation will continue to wear down any of the rough spots contained in these regional trading agreements and we should welcome them for this reason.

Some of these circles will evolve closer together. CER could become the basic unit of a South Pacific community, which in turn could bring that circle of influence to bear inside ASEAN and APEC. These units will gather influence and thus more leverage within the wider forums.

We in the South Pacific should assist in building a regional identity. New Zealand is a proud sovereign Pacific state. Independence through interdependence is how New Zealand can best promote its interests into the next century. We can engage and win at every level of international activity. We are a threat to no one but ourselves. We can in a modest, practical way advance our interests with integrity and without geographical envy or malice.

In a single lifetime we have moved from the comfort of empire through depression, world wars, and Cold War stand-offs to see former colonies and recipients of foreign aid eclipse New Zealand in terms of living standards.

The role of leaders is to put before the people future dangers, opportunities, options and solutions. This is frequently uncomfortable. But the future is to be faced, not feared. We have much to offer, much to lose and everything to gain.

It's more comfortable to live in the past. But I've seen the past. It didn't work.

In this book I hope I have left 'no shins unkicked'. Indeed, that was my original working title.

CHAPTER ONE

The Information Age: Glimpses of the Future

A quick stroke of a key, and she places her order to purchase some fabulous new household furniture. The lucky buyer discovered the speciality furniture company while browsing the Internet, hoping to find just the perfect room additions, unavailable in the retail stores to which her well-meaning spouse had dragged her. The best part of the purchase: the 'custom' design. She had engaged in an on-line 'conversation' with one of the company's marketing representatives. He had used his own Internet connection to convey her wishes to a designer, who just happened to be sitting on a beach in a remote Caribbean location.

He would spend some time reflecting upon the buyer's dream room, and, using his talent and the inspiration of the sunset, would draw up sketches and specifications to suit her needs. As he worked he accessed a large computer mainframe in Pittsburgh. The furniture design software on the mainframe was quite remarkable, designed specifically for this business by an employee living in Australia (where none of the company's business had ever been done).

In fact, the computer itself did a lot of the work the designer would have done himself some years back, like assessing potential design flaws, automatically calculating material requirements, and determining the proper architectural aspects for safety and durability. The designer, happily, was left to his art. But some of his ideas were refined by accessing a large database of furniture design reports and patent filings, part of which he downloaded from the Pittsburgh computer for reference.

When finished with his work, the designer would communicate his plans electronically to craftsmen in the European countryside, who through their laptops, and tying into the mainframe computer services, would serve as consultants to workers at a large factory in an Asian city, where the furniture would be produced. The craftsmen might even have a video-conference from time to time. The customer paid for the purchase by a charge to her 'e-money' account, and all the other cross-border transfers were paid for in the same way, even among the related companies involved in the transaction.[1]

Nothing will ever be the same, and there is no going back. Change is being forced upon us as we enter a new age: the information age. At the moment we are experiencing painful birth pangs. Things are moving more swiftly than our institutions, and in some case our ethics, can cope. But let me just give you some raw facts about what's happening out there in the age of information technology:

- Information technology (IT) industries are growing at double the rate of overall economies.
- Investment in IT now represents 45 per cent of all business equipment investment in the US.
- Declining prices for IT investments have helped lower global inflation.
- The amount of business written on the Internet doubles every 100 days.
- 65,000 new pages go on the Internet every hour; 1.5 million per day.
- There are 320 million pages today; there will be 3 billion within two years.
- Internet business will reach $300 billion within a decade.
- In 1980 phone conversations travelled over copper wires, which carried less than one page of information per second. Now a strand of optical fibre as thin as a human hair can transmit in a second the equivalent of 90,000 volumes of the *Encyclopedia Britannica*. One pound of fibreoptics can shift more information that one ton of copper.
- By 2002, an armada of low-orbit satellites will bring high-bandwidth communications to businesses, schools and individuals.
- It took radio 38 years to reach 50 million people. It took 13 years for TV to reach that number. It took 16 years for the personal computer to reach 50 million people. The Internet crossed the line in four years, with one billion users predicted in 2005.[2]

Most people would guess that the most widely used language would be English or Chinese. They would be wrong. Computers now have more conversations *each day* than all the collective conversations between our species since time began.

The information revolution provides freedoms not imagined. My publisher, David Elworthy from Shoal Bay Press, told me that on a trip to the US this year he was introduced to the latest advance in publishing. IBM technology can be used to provide on-demand book printing. Customers request a book from computer files held by the printer, the computer/printer goes to work and in a few minutes out pops a complete, printed, bound book with a full-colour soft cover. Print runs can be reduced to one copy. It is mostly used at this stage for out-of-print titles, but the implications are intriguing. No storage? No transport costs? No inventory? No bookshops? No libraries? No over-runs? No remainder sales? No trouble. Saves energy and trees! This must help the book consumer, cut costs and give new authors and small publishers opportunities never imagined a few years, or even months, ago.

This is just 'time management' taken to its ultimate – or maybe one day we will have books printed in our homes. Of course we can read them on the Internet, but there's still something special about a book.

Many major hotels now offer a great service to customers who wish to read their home-town newspapers: they simply print them off the Internet and push them under their bedroom doors.

Time magazine in 1997 convened a distinguished panel at the annual World Economic Forum in Switzerland who predicted that the art and practice of government would never be the same. They all foresaw a new epoch of governance with inevitable changes, most too new and too enormous to comprehend fully.

'It's a little bit like standing in the middle of a landed aristocratic gathering in 1500,' said Newt Gingrich, Speaker of the US House of Representatives, 'and describing the impact of the printing press, and having all the aristocrats say, "Well, none of us learned how to read. That's why we hire scribes." '[3]

Those scribes of old, so loyal to their lords, have become armies of taxpaying citizens with Internet accounts. It's a whole new ball game. Now, in theory at least, whole populations will have direct access to information without waiting for it to be filtered through a government, or the media – or even filtered at all. That raises all sorts of issues for the way leaders deal with their people. As Kofi Annan, United Nations Secretary General, said: 'If you are into control, it's frightening. This thing cannot stop.'[4]

The cost of this opening of the information floodgates will be felt particularly by governments with hitherto closed economies which, to capture the blessings of growth, need to open these economies fully to the outside world. Democracy and freedom will advance, not contract, with globalisation. Open economies eventually force open political systems. That's why tyrants fear information. They fear the people because knowledge is power.

If knowledge is power, how much can we predict of what will happen? Just how much of a shock does the future hold? In the past, we have missed the boat a bit with predictions about some of the great inventions. Thomas Edison thought the phonograph would be mainly used for recording people's wills and perhaps some office dictation. He had no inkling that his invention would bring beautiful music to the ordinary people.

A British parliamentary select committee considered Edison's lamp and thought it 'good enough for our transatlantic friends, but unworthy of the attention of practical or scientific means'.

The Mercedes motor company in 1903 envisaged that 'there will never be more than a million cars worldwide. It's implausible that more than a million artisans would be trainable as chauffeurs.'

Not quite as embarrassing as the US Commissioner of Patents, Charles H. Duell, who said in 1897: 'Everything that can be invented has been invented.'

Or a Western Union memo in 1876, which confidently asserted: 'This "telephone" has too many shortcomings to be seriously considered as a means of communication. The device is inherently of no value to us.' They turned down an opportunity to purchase Alexander Graham Bell's struggling company for $100,000, saying, "What use could this company make of an electrical toy?"'

The powers of governments over traditional areas of the economy will be transformed by the new logic of the Internet. Extraterritorial regulatory power will collapse. Jurisdictions will devolve. The structure of firms will change, and so will the nature of work and employment.

Some have suggested that the information age will spell the end of the nation state. In 1795 Immanuel Kant's essay *Perpetual Peace* and later Karl Marx's *Withering of the State* suggested that the nation state would ultimately become almost irrelevant. Many today agree with them. But that's not the way I see it. The nation state is certainly changing, but I believe will ultimately be strengthened by that changes that await us.

I agree with management guru and author Peter Drucker when he suggests that

> ... there is no other institution capable of political integration and effective membership in the world's political community. In all probability, therefore, the nation state will survive the globalisation of the economy and the information revolution that accompanies it. But, it will be a greatly changed nation state, especially in domestic fiscal and monetary policies, foreign economic policies, control of international business, and, perhaps, in its conduct of war.

Drucker goes on to speak of the changes that lie ahead in the financial cyber-marketplace.

> The volume of world money is so gigantic that its movements in and out of a currency have far greater impact than the flows of financing, trade or investment. In one day, as much of this virtual money may be traded as the

entire world needs to finance trade and investment for a year. This virtual money has total mobility because it serves no economic function. Billions of it can be switched from one currency to another by a trader pushing a few buttons on a keyboard ...

Business will live in a borderless world, technology will enable managers to speak and fax in any language and you will pay for services in cyberspace, outside the jurisdiction of nation states. The tax base will shrink dramatically. Shopping will become easier and more competitive. Tourists on the Internet can't be stopped and will choose from wherever they want. Suits [can be] made to measure in Thailand, and couriered anywhere. Distance education means tutorials prepared and read in Oxford can be received anywhere.

Already the military have experimented with virtual surgery. It was the US military that invented the Internet as an alternative information system if conventional systems were disabled. Men wounded on the battlefield will be operated via satellite by a team of New York specialists.

Lord William Rees-Mogg and James Davidson in *The Sovereign Individual* tell us that

... General Electric has redesigned magnetic resonance machines so that they can be used for treatment as well as diagnosis ... Instead of taking an image and then performing surgery in the light of that image, the surgeon will be able to see what he is doing as he does it. Instead of having to make large incisions with scalpels, the surgeon will make micro incisions with probes, and will be able to see what the probes reveal as he operates. He will perform the surgery from the image rather than by looking directly into the body. In principle, the probes will be operable from a distance. They will be able to destroy tumours with laser or cryogenic – heating or freezing – devices of great precision.

Some researchers believe that the knife for soft-tissue surgery may be looked back on as an obsolete relic by 2010. A lot of fear, and much of the aftershock, will be taken out or surgery if that is true ... Operations that now take hours to perform, and have to be followed by days or weeks in hospital, will take only half an hour, and may not require hospitalisation at all. Indeed, the surgeon and the patient may never even be in the same room.

What is this going to do to our hospitals? To the surgeons who work in them? To the public who march to save these institutions they adore and trust?

Information-age hospitals and medicine will be as different as industrial-age medicine was from medieval witchcraft. Curiously, the final bastion of industrial-age factory-type assembly-line manufacturing will be in education, where students still sit around a teacher in a room as they have for hundreds of years. Chalk has given way to overhead projectors, but the Taylor and Ford system of the assembly line still dominates and intimidates.

Sure, we will always need teachers face to face, but it is technically possible for the best history or maths teacher to be beamed into every classroom and have her backed up by assistants in the room. In rural areas of South Australia, a state larger than Texas, distance education is beamed out so that the pupils can see the teacher, but the teacher can also see and interact with the pupils.

Hundreds, even thousands of TV and radio stations will come on line through new satellite technology. We face the dreary prospect of a dedicated Spice Girls TV and radio channel through the Internet or on your radio and TV set of the future. Or perhaps 'virtual reality' trips through museums and history. Imagine the implications for copyright law.

The globalisation of commerce obviously means big headaches ahead for treasuries, and revenue and tax gatherers, and will force them to co-operate even further. Our Caribbean furniture designer in the example that opened this chapter

> … provides his services from a tax-friendly jurisdiction, but his services are received at various locations throughout the world. Yet only his Caribbean paradise would have the right to tax the designer's compensation, no doubt a premium compensation reflecting his talents and skills. So, with no change in traditional tax concepts, a company might locate all its skilled personnel in a tax haven, and provide consulting services to high-tax European countries, without ever creating a permanent establishment. Once again, the communications revolution can be seen as putting pressure on the traditional concept of residence-based taxation.[5]

It's tough enough plugging tax loopholes under present technologies on a domestic basis. Every year Cabinet pores over documents and tax amendments, realising that last year's efforts to plug loopholes have become unstuck again. New Zealand tax laws are over 3000 pages and getting longer, especially now a taskforce has attempted to simplify the procedures. How can single governments alone tax or even know or keep up with the new form of transactions? What about money laundering and international crime?

International transactions on the foreign exchange markets exceed $NZ2000 billion per day. The power of this mega-market is awesome. Every day the financial markets vote in their assessment of a nation's economic virtue. When

Indonesia's and Malaysia's currency crashed it wasn't because they were suddenly 50 per cent less competent or 50 per cent less capable or 50 per cent less wealthy. The financial markets work on a basket of rumours and intuition and are in the main correct in their responses.

But in these new days of rapid and overwhelming information the reef fish swim together, the better for collective protection, but oblivious of their direction. Group panic enters – no one wants to be left behind. The reef fish theory of group behaviour is common to the most primitive species in the lagoon and the most sophisticated Wall Street yuppie.

Even the capable and conservative chairman of the US Federal Reserve, Alan Greenspan, was moved to comment:

> The global financial system has been evolving rapidly in recent years. New technology has radically reduced the costs of borrowing and lending across traditional national borders, facilitating the development of new instruments and drawing in new players. One result has been a massive increase in capital flows. Information is transmitted instantaneously around the world, and huge shifts in the supply and demand for funds naturally follow.
>
> This burgeoning global system has been demonstrated to be a highly efficient structure that has significantly facilitated cross-border trade in goods and services and, accordingly, has made a substantial contribution to standards of living worldwide. Its efficiency exposes and punishes underlying economic weakness swiftly and decisively. Regrettably, it also appears to have facilitated the transmission of disturbances far more effectively than ever before. The crisis in Mexico several years ago was the first such episode associated with our high-tech international financial system. The current Asian crisis is the second.
>
> The sharp exchange rate changes in East Asia in recent months, as similar instances elsewhere, do not appear to have resulted wholly from a measured judgement that fundamental forces have turned appreciably more adverse. More likely, its root is a process that is neither measured nor rational, [but] one based on a visceral, engulfing fear. The exchange rate changes appears the consequences, not of the accumulation of new knowledge of a deterioration in fundamentals, but of its opposite: the onset of uncertainties that destroy previous understandings of the way the world works. That has induced massive disengagements of investors and declines in Asian currencies that have no tie to reality. In all aspects of life, when confronted with uncertainty, people tend to withdraw …
>
> These two recent crisis episodes have afforded us increasing insights into the dynamics of the evolving international financial system, though there is much we do not yet understand …[6]

We are getting accustomed to eftpos and an increasingly cashless society. The total number of non-cash payments in New Zealand amounts to 4.25 million transactions through banks each day – more than a billion a year. Cyber-money means cash and investment are increasingly being denationalised, but protectionism will become less and less effective as a national strategy. In a way it will be a throwback to the times before states controlled and issued currencies. Given that economic growth can be directly related to economic freedom, what will this mean?

The new cyber-economy abolishes the tyranny of place and language; distance becomes time: milliseconds not miles. Location will become meaningless and there will be a shrinking role for organisations, businesses, politicians, unions and researchers that exist within strictly national boundaries, and an expanded role for those that function globally. If a firm in Timaru wanted an accountant or typist in days past, that person had to drive to work. Now the accountant may live in Bengal, or Bucharest, or in the Coromandel.

John Naisbitt has written several bestsellers predicting what he calls 'Megatrends'. In 1984 he suggested the 1990s would be shaped by the following trends:

1. Industrial society   →   information society
2. Forced technology   →   high tech/high touch
3. National economy   →   world economy
4. Short term   →   long term
5. Centralisation   →   decentralisation
6. Institutional help   →   self-help
7. Representative democracy →   participatory democracy
8. Hierarchies   →   networking
9. North   →   south
10. Either/or   →   multiple option[7]

As we enter this new millennium Naisbitt and co-author Patricia Aburdene predict that the overarching trends influencing our lives will be:

1. The booming global economy of the 1990s
2. A renaissance in the arts
3. The emergence of free-market socialism
4. Global lifestyles and cultural nationalism
5. The privatisation of the welfare state
6. The rise of the Pacific Rim

7. The decade of women in leadership
8. The age of biology
9. The religious revival of the new millennium
10. The triumph of the individual[8]

With the cyber-economy comes a global lifestyle. Already no passports are necessary within an expanded Europe. Marco Polo earned a place in history for his travels. Now, over 1.5 million people cross national boundaries every day.

Technophobia swept the world when scientists cloned Dolly the Sheep. The threat to New Zealand's conventional markets will not come through quantitative restrictions, or tariffs, but from the new biotechnological industry of the future. It's not science fiction any more. Today's sheep, cattle, kiwifruit and pine trees are not like their ancestors of generations ago. They have been bred into new products. Test-tube tomatoes are with us. Pharmaceuticals from plants and plants from pharmaceuticals! A caffeine-free coffee plant has been developed at the University of Hawaii in Manoa. I wonder how much work has been done by the tobacco companies to produce a nicotine-free tobacco?

Every week a report surfaces about scientists cloning animals or plants, or growing human body parts in host animals for transplant. A plant biologist in Washington has developed the technology for making plastic from a mustard plant, meaning a biological plastics industry will be a commercial reality. The *Evening Post* in April 1998 reported that a six-year-old British girl was to fly to the United States to undergo the world's first surgical operation to grow a new ear. Massachusetts surgeons believed they could grow a new ear for her using cells from her existing left ear.

In Australia, scientists are developing ways to grow naturally coloured cotton, as dying cotton is the most polluting part of preparing that product for sale. Seems we can soon expect to see fields of blue, black, red and white cotton plants. The drive for 'greener', more environmentally sound processes is fuelling all sorts of hitherto undreamed-of innovations. Scientists have already designed a micro-organism that can reduce contaminants by 80 per cent and may in the future clean radioactive waste.

Biotechnology has got ahead of a consensus and our capacity to deal with the ethical issues involved. Domestic and international law lags behind the imagination and genius of invention. The predictable response from those fearful of change and those whose interests are threatened will be to call for a halt. But as we know, that is just not possible. We have to evolve ways of dealing with and handling the change that is upon us, and managing it to our collective advantage.

Terrorism and the waging of war will take on a new face in the information age.

Terrorist viruses put into computer systems could disable airlines, water, power and hospital supplies. This opens up a new world of terrorist possibilities and the costs of protection will rocket. Teenage hackers periodically crash into top-secret Pentagon files. Experts fear that determined terrorists could destroy the Olympic Games by computer disruptions. A new form of commercial and personal blackmail and extortion will emerge.

Auckland was paralysed because of a major accidental power fault. Imagine if something similar were done on purpose?

In April this year US intelligence officials revealed evidence of what they called the first known attack by a terrorist group on a target country's computer systems. An offshoot of the Tamil Tigers is believed to have launched a form of 'information systems terrorism' consisting of mass email 'bombings' aimed at countering US propaganda.

Releasing gas in an underground system is personally dangerous and leaves fingerprints. Mostly the perpetrators are caught. But re-routing trains by hijacking computer systems is much more anonymous – and potentially much more deadly.

In response to these threats, security will soon be the fastest-growing industry outside technology and entertainment.

Just as the invention of the nuclear bomb changed war and disrupted the basis of global power forever because we had at last discovered the ability to kill everyone, humans have at their disposal through the new information age the technical skills to destabilise, by mistake or at will, the security and stability of nation states. This is the biggest threat to the integrity of the sovereign state since man mounted a horse, or lifted a sail, or invented gunpowder.

But we are all in this together. History tells us that we can all win: that in the main the story of our civilisation is one of progress. All that's different this time is that the speed of things has accelerated. The horse, then the sail, steam, rail, oil, diesel, aircraft, jets then space, now cyber-space – that's history.

How do we ensure we move peacefully into this new age, without the violence, pain, unemployment and poverty that have accompanied other major historic global changes? This will be the real test of policymakers who look beyond today and beyond a single parliamentary term or annual balance sheet. And one thing is for certain: no one country can do it alone. It will take bold internationalist policies abroad as well as brave domestic programmes at home.

CHAPTER TWO

Fortune Favours the Brave

Education makes a people easy to lead, but difficult to drive; easy to govern but impossible to enslave. – Lord Brougham (1778-1868)

OVER THE PAST two decades it has become clear that nations that embrace the global economy prosper and those that don't falter, fail and fall behind. Compare Singapore with Burma, Belgium with Russia. It's not just a matter of national resources. Nor is it a new phenomenon. The march of civilisation has been a story of vibrant, often violent, internationalism by daring explorers and traders, of colonial conquest and the exchange of ideas and products. Inward-looking societies have perished or limped behind as history and progress strode over or around them. Why?

Our distant cousins, the apes, lived in family tribes, as did our prehistoric relatives. The family tribe was for millions of years the basic political and social unit. Going beyond this structure took a relatively few thousand years. Over the 12,000 years of mankind's most rapid march we separated into two types of existence: hunter-gatherers on the one hand, and those who domesticated animals and crops on the other.

The latter, the efficient farmers, began to grow and store food. They domesticated animals. There arose the first permanent villages, the most basic collective social unit. Here was a society that did not live by self-sufficiency, that traded its surplus grain or pottery for other things it wanted but did not produce: the beginnings of economic specialisation.

Specialisation led to the development of the basic political, religious and social structures. In short, civil organisation. Increasing wealth and 'surplus' time allowed expeditions in search of riches and new technologies, ideas, crops and animals, which in turn refined specialisation, improved living standards and created a new world in which the ideas of others could be utilised.

If we accept that specialisation and the division of labour kick-started civilisation, it was to take our species millennia to create the intellectual underpinning of that ancient and fruitful discovery. Indeed, it was not until 1772 that one David Ricardo, the son of a Dutch banker, a multi-millionaire and

Radical MP in Westminster, was able to formulate what is perhaps the best-established, though quite subtle, of observations: the theory of comparative advantage. He argued that specialisation at level of the group, not just the individual, was the basis of economic success. Some assume that the logical extension of this is that the most efficient nation or company would consume the whole market, but this ignores the competitive advantage afforded by innovation, new product ranges and consumer emotion.

Swapping and trading products is as old as time. It reduces risk of shortage; it's a more efficient use of resources. The old arguments about divisions of labour apply equally between countries, tribes and groups.

Ricardo just explained what our forefathers were doing anyway. The law of comparative advantage is one of the ecological aces that defines and separates our species.

Man has always been curious and/or hungry enough to look and wonder what was beyond the horizon. It's in the nature of our species. People were on the move before nations' boundaries were drawn, and war and conquest became inevitable. In this and other areas farmers and settlers had an advantage over the more primitive hunter-gatherers. Technology and invention accelerated urbanisation and surplus rural labour, which could form the basis of full-time standing armies. Their supply lines became stretched. This was also a lesson of the New Zealand land wars, Maori against the Crown. The hunter-gatherers, with their focus firmly on day-to-day survival, could not maintain troops in the field for long periods of time.

Islamic traders sailed from Africa to Asia and India, taking with them ideas and culture, as well as commercial products. Their society prospered. The Ottoman and Islamic empires stretched from North Africa across the southern Mediterranean to the gates of Vienna until they were stopped by a Europe finally united by fear, the sword and cavalry of Christendom.

Jared Diamond's book *Guns, Germs and Steel*, which he describes as 'a short history of everybody for the last 13,000 years', examines why some continents and races expanded and exploded beyond their valleys and shores while others did not.

China had great trading ships twice the size of Columbus's puny fleet that sailed and traded with India, Africa and the Islamic world. One fleet had a crew of over 20,000 men. China enjoyed the benefits of magnetic compasses, drills, gunpowder, fine silks and cloth, medicine, law and civilisation's largest irrigation system centuries before Britons learnt that coal was a source of energy. Why did this progress stop? Why did the nation that discovered how to manufacture iron and rotate crops not remain the premier economic and organised society?

The answer is simple: politics. A leadership battle was won by those who looked inwards. It was considered that the 'centre of the world' need not look elsewhere for inspiration. Economic and social chauvinism and nationalistic isolationism starved Chinese society of ideas and innovation.

During the reunification ceremony in Hong Kong last year I remarked to a senior Chinese official that it was obvious China was destined to be the other superpower. He replied that China had always been the most powerful nation on earth, except for the past 200 years, which had been an aberration.

Throughout history outward-looking peoples and leaders have prospered and won, while inward-looking peoples and leaders have lost and their people's prosperity has suffered.

The enterprising Portuguese adventurer Vasco da Gama, who in the 15th century became the first European to sail around the southern tip of Africa, picked up a pilot from the Kenyan coast who took him to India. Tiny Portugal and Holland in time became great trading nations. Holland is still a great trading nation, the world's biggest exporter of tobacco products and a great oil exporter. Yet none of these products is gathered locally. Portugal, on the other hand, retreated because inward-looking leaders and fascism pulled it back from the front line of open and curious societies.

Japan, within 60 years of the arrival of Portuguese vessels armed with a new weapon (guns), improved on those weapons and owned more and better guns than any country in the world. Why did they surrender this technology for over 100 years until Commander Perry's gunboats forced them to do an about-turn? Because the ruling class, the Samurai, were a warrior class and warfare was conducted by gentlemen who, one to one, after much grace, ritual and speeches, did battle. When peasant soldiers discovered that guns were a great equaliser, laws were passed in Japan restricting their use. Equality and the democratisation of power are always resisted by those who enjoy its monopoly at any one time.

Genghis Khan swept all before him and his army was poised to take Europe. But his untimely death put paid to this scheme because of the cultural (i.e. political) requirement that he be buried in his homeland. This meant the withdrawal of the greatest and most effective military force of its time.

A factor that gave an advantage to European invaders was, ironically, disease. Urbanisation and the domestication of animals (unknown at the stage in the Americas or Africa) created most unhealthy environments. Plagues and diseases spread, wiping out huge numbers of people and stock. But after a while people built up immunity to these fearful diseases, and civilisation was further promoted by the introduction of collective solutions to the problems of sewerage and water supply. These factors gave Europeans a deadly advantage in the looming battles of colonialism and the invasion of lands not immune to such plagues.

It is true that steel, horsepower and gunpowder allowed the tiny Spanish army of Cortez, some few hundred in number, to defeat Indian armies of tens of thousands in the 16th century. But it was smallpox, influenza and other diseases, to which Europeans were in the main immune, that wrought the most destruction. By 1618 the local population of 20 million had dropped to under 2 million. The Indian population in North America declined by 95 per cent in the 200 years after Columbus's arrival.

Captain Cook's visit to Hawaii and the typhoid and smallpox epidemics that followed cut the island's population from 500,000 to 70,000.

European settlers in North America wiped out countless native Indians by deliberately giving them blankets from smallpox victims in one of the first examples of germ warfare. At last now we have international treaties on germ warfare that all but the rogue nations have signed.

In New Zealand influenza killed more Maori than the Queen's rifles. It took its toll also on European colonists, but not to nearly the same extent. The Bible, bayonets, booze and bank managers did the rest.

The immunities the European colonists developed in part dictated where they successfully settled in great numbers, in environments where their animals from moderate European climates, cattle, sheep and horses, could prosper. North America but not central Africa; Australia but not Papua New Guinea.

Thus we have learnt that the 'self-sufficient' state is doomed to fail. By its very nature it is isolationist, insular and inward-looking. The world has been shaped by the cross-pollination of ideas and technologies. In the pursuit of progress the slow and insular have always paid a price and gone the way of the dodo.

New Zealanders once understood this. Bob Semple and Labour in the 1930s acknowledged that truth, and in a blaze of publicity Semple used the first bulldozer to grind and smash wheelbarrows, promising to save the sweat and blood of the working man. This at the height of the Great Depression, when unemployment had reached historic levels and the very existence of capitalism was under threat. (Reactionaries who oppose new technology now would no doubt have opposed the wheelbarrows, arguing that teaspoons would have created more jobs in road-building. One Labour MP in caucus recently asked me to guarantee no more jobs would be lost in Telecom, and the Alliance political leadership periodically win headlines suggesting there will be more bank layoffs.)

The United States invented the transistor, but its commercial leaders were content with their old valve technology and easy profits. The new technology passed to Japan, as eventually did market dominance. The Islamic world acquired Chinese paper-making technologies after the battle of Talas River in 751 AD, by taking paper-making prisoners. Silkworms were smuggled from Asia to the Middle East in 550 AD in an early example of industrial espionage.

Europe admired and prized Chinese porcelain for several hundred years before they managed to duplicate the process. We still call such products household 'china'. Department stores still have counters selling 'manchester'. Manchester was the premier cotton-weaving capital when Britain ruled the waves and waived the economic rules.

Migration throughout history has also fostered innovation and change. When the French expelled the Huguenots, 200,000 of them spread their glass and clothing techniques over all of Europe. Hitler expelled Jewish scientists from Nazi Germany, probably denying himself the atomic bomb that could have given him global dominance. New Zealand gained a wine industry from Croatia and a dairy industry from Denmark. A handful of Jewish wartime and pre-war refugees changed New Zealand's economic, social and civil life when they excelled in business, the law and the arts.

Each group of migrants has bought skills, enterprise, sweat and ideas. In 30 years 20 million migrants arrived in the United States, catapulting that country to the front rank of nations. The initiatives they founded eventually outshone many industries in their homelands. The Kodak empire was established by German immigrants, and Germany led the cinematic world until it exiled its Jewish expertise, which regrouped in Hollywood. Switzerland prospered through the banking and watchmaking skills of refugees.

Nations that are open to the immigration of people, products and ideas do better in the long run. Tsarist and Stalinist Russia, and imperial and Maoist China, were opposing ideologies, but all practised inward-looking arrogance, convinced they were superior and didn't need the ideas of decadent outsiders. All failed their people.

The truly great leaders in history have been internationalists, curious about the world. They have expanded their intellectual horizons, through trade, the arts, science and religion. Some have done it peacefully, others by force. They have taken their people out of sullen domestic introspection to a wider plain and more open roads. The inward-looking, those who have thought their civilisation was and is the pinnacle of human endeavour and history, ended up withering and perishing.

The success of the West and then Japan has been in such openness. Openness to ideas, to the competition of products and services, and to the expansion of their people's vision. They lifted rather than lowered their people's sights; they were the modernisers of history and changed their nations' directions.

Similarly, Nelson Mandela led his people forward. Mindful of the past and injustices that needed to be corrected, he was nevertheless open to the best the new world can offer. He rejected tribalism and advanced culture and commerce.

Peter the Great took Russia from a medieval, superstitious primitive society to the front line of European nations of the day. He was brutal but brilliant and thirsty for knowledge. He was the first Russian tsar to travel beyond his nation's boundary. He worked in shipyards, steel factories, hospitals, employing hated foreigners to modernise his nation. He learnt to sail so he could develop a Russian navy, and later built a new capital, St Petersburg, a naval base that looked west, not east. He stripped the religious leaders not only of their power but of their beards and flowing garments. By this modernisation, no longer were the Swedes, Poles and Turks a threat to his people. Literacy rose, infant mortality dropped and Russia prospered.

Alas, Peter's heirs believed the old propaganda, and saw themselves as having divine rights as God's representatives. They stopped the modernisation programmes. God had made Peter curious but his heirs were not. They in turn perished, to be replaced by another elite who were equally convinced of the rightness of their cause. The Union of Soviet Socialist Republics was in the end so little different to the Russia of the last tsars.

China's experience is horribly similar: both countries have a recent history of closed economies, closed-minded, autocratic and cruel leaders who provoked, by their ignorance, communist revolutions. These revolutions produced leaders like Mao Zedong and Joseph Stalin, who became the new emperors, who burnt books, tried to ban sparrows, murdered millions and drove their society backwards by generations.

In the 1990s Deng Xiaoping in China and Mikhail Gorbachev in the Soviet Union strove to open up their respective economies and societies. They knew Marxism had failed. Deng sought economic liberalisation ahead of political liberation; Gorbachev did things the other way around.

Deng's famous phrase in defence of open investment and new ideas, 'it doesn't matter if the cat is black or white, so long as it catches the mice', provided the impetus for economic freedom that has seen Chinese people recently enjoy unprecedented rises in living standards. Millions are on the move to the southern growth areas. Why? People want a better future. Famine is no longer a daily danger. Why? People produce more if they own their products. Sure, it's imperfect, dangerous still, but China will surely be the next superpower and within a lifetime will have a larger economy than the US and Japan combined.

Do they have further still to go? Yes. Could it all come unstuck? Of course. History is never a straight line.

The great Frenchman Robert Schuman was conscripted into the German army in the First World War and worked with the Resistance during the Second World War. Then, as Prime Minister of France and later Foreign Minister his patience and vision led him to promote the Monnet plan for a European coal and steel community. The proposal was that coal and steel resources in Western Europe be pooled and administered by both the national states and by a pan-European authority, with the objective of gradually reducing tariffs in these heavy industries. A bold first step towards European integration.

Schuman and Monnet were visionaries who set in train the steps that have created what idealistic men and women (and quite a few villains) have dreamed of for centuries, a European Union. The world is safer, stronger and better because of this. The great white tribes of Europe are mainly at peace. We have been dragged into their dreadful civil wars twice this century. This is now less likely, barring possible tribal outbreaks.

Kemal Ataturk was another great leader who transformed his country. Ataturk gave women in Turkey equal rights, removed the power of the high priests of Islam, changed the dress of the day. He looked to Europe, and called together the scholars, religious leaders and politicians, saying he wanted a new Latin alphabet to replace the Arabic alphabet. When he was told it would take three years he said: 'Well, you had better leave now, you have wasted 30 months already.' Turkey is now firmly anchored in the West, an important middle power that so far has survived the historic and cultural test of being sandwiched between Europe and the East.

What did those leaders who have been canonised by their people have in common? Okay, yes, absolute power. But besides that, they had a curiosity about the outside world, a determination to utilise the best the world had to offer and the courage to break with the past in that process. They broke the religious straightjackets of their nations. They respected their history and culture and at the same time drove towards a new age.

Historian J.H. Elliott composed an epitaph to the decline of imperial Spain during the 17th century:

> Heirs to a society which had overinvested in empire, and surrounded by the increasingly shabby remnants of a dwindling inheritance, they could not bring themselves at the moment of crisis to surrender their memories and alter the antique pattern of their lives. At a time when the face of Europe was altering more rapidly that ever before, the country that had once been its leading power proved to be lacking the essential ingredient for survival – the willingness to change.

Throughout history those with power have often tried to retain it through force and control, resisting change at all costs. At the height of the feudal age the churches were in charge, but they faced competition from new ideas and new technologies.

It was the invention of the printing press that led to people's liberation from the control of the churches, which hitherto had monopolised the spread of information. The printing press offered an opportunity for the publication of new ideas. Some 10 million books were printed in the last decade of the 15th century, and so-called subversive ideas flourished. In the West the church was unsuccessful in suppressing this new technology (not for want of trying), but in China those with power succeeded, thus helping freeze that nation's progress centuries ago.

Increasing literacy in the West further eroded the control of the church and its partners, the feudal lords, and the medieval view of the world was soon under serious threat. The printing press changed the face of society forever by freeing up the monopoly of information.

Canon law had been very useful to the churches in providing legal protection for their power (just as import controls and tariffs do for the powerful interests and their political delegates today). The rule about eating fish on Fridays was based on church control of the major fishing fleet, and the fact that it suited to ensure a demand for the product at a low time in the week. Manufacturers who tried to source textiles from a cheaper Turkish wholesaler were threatened with excommunication. Even the monopoly on marrying people was a good moneyspinner for a time. Devotion to feudal lords was peasant insurance, but devotion to the church was a longer-term guarantee.

The church came to be universally despised, its leadership seen as corrupt, self-serving and at odds with its own morals and unable to protect and maintain the people's economic and social position. Change was forced upon it.

Today's political leaders can no more hold the line and preserve the present, as we slip into a new economic and social epoch, than the European princes and popes could stop the historic avalanche of change that swept their world as the industrial age arrived. Most of the arguments between contemporary left and right have the same relevance as the old arguments between Protestants and Catholics in Europe centuries ago.

Civilisations, nations and societies that stand still are eclipsed. The lesson of history is that political leadership that tries to retain power by the use of force and by manipulating fear succeeds only at great cost and for a short time. Such civilisations and societies have always perished or gone into decline.

We all want the best the world can offer in medicine when we are sick. We all treasure ancient and new literature. Shakespeare and Mickey Mouse, X-rays and penicillin know no national boundaries drawn up by politicians.

The true nationalist and patriot is also an internationalist. This is not a contradiction. No people are more proud and independent than the 'swatched-on' Swiss or the steely, sophisticated, ball-bearing Swedes. They have delivered the highest levels of living standards to their peoples. Like the sturdy Dutch, Singaporean and Hong Kong Chinese, they are aggressive internationalists in the economic sense, as well as in their commitment to co-operation among nations.

CHAPTER THREE

Co-operation, Reciprocity and Democracy: The Human Way

If a free society cannot help the many who are poor,
it cannot save the few who are rich. – John F. Kennedy

MAYBE THE NEED of our species to expand, control, record history, store grain and accumulate wealth goes much deeper than political and economic theory. Perhaps at its base lies an evolutionary answer. Perhaps that's what defines and makes our species different. In the main we enjoy and are enriched by change and new experiences. Isn't that what travel, books and cinema are all about?

Evolutionary biologists and historians write of a human 'selfish gene'. Central to this theory is the argument that people do not do things solely for the good of themselves or their group, but for the benefit of future generations. Genetic nepotism, the determination to ensure the survival of the species, is seen as the source of ambition, industry and drive.

As Matt Ridley says in his book, *The Origins of Virtue*, none of our ancestors died celibate.

If we accept absolute rationalism we become what Robert Wright termed 'rational fools'. There is a morality, whether you accept the selfish gene theory or a more biblical interpretation of the point and purpose of our species. The Ten Commandments are rational as well as commonsense, and these principles applied more widely become the basis of good governance. The biblical theories of reciprocal treatment being the basis of a just life are as profound for nations as they are for individuals.

All societies have their own moral structures, but all religions and cultures are based loosely on the concept of reciprocal treatment: you treat others as you would like to be treated yourself.

And very early on man learnt that the basis of reciprocity is co-operation. No one can survive alone. History and evolution teach us that one and one can make three when we co-operate. It's called synergy.

Said Adam Smith:

Each animal is still obliged to support and defend itself, separately and in-dependently, and derives no sort of advantage from that variety of talents with which nature has distinguished its fellows. Among men, on the contrary, the most dissimilar geniuses are of use to one another; the different produces of their respective talents, by the general disposition to truck, barter and exchange, being brought, as it were, into a common stock, where every man may purchase whatever part of the produce of the other men's talents he has occasion for.[1]

Both Smith and Darwin have been adopted by economic and social extremists to justify racist and criminally exploitative policies as being the natural order of things. But most have not studied Smith's later work, *The Theory of Moral Sentiments*, in which he argued that

> ... benevolence is inadequate for the task of building co-operation in a large society, because we are irredeemably biased in our benevolence to relatives and close friends; a society built on benevolence would be riddled with nepotism. Between strangers, the invisible hand of the market, distributing selfish ambitions, is fairer.[2]

The division of labour marked our species as different. No one man alone can kill and eat a mammoth. It was an early form of co-operation for the public good. In Chapter 2, I looked at how specialisation created the opportunity for tribes to become states. Adam Smith was the first to intellectually identify the division of labour as making human society more than the sum of its parts.

In the opening chapter of his landmark book *An Inquiry into the Nature and Causes of the Wealth of Nations* he chose to illustrate the point with the example of a pin-maker. Somebody not trained in pin-making could probably make only one pin a day, and even when practised would probably be able to make only 20 or so. Yet, by dividing labour between pin-makers and non-pin-makers and by further dividing the task of pin manufacture between a number of specialist trades, we vastly increase the number of pins that can be made by each person. Ten people in a pin factory could produce 48,000 pins a day. To buy 20 pins from such a factory therefore costs only 1/240 of a man-day, whereas it would have taken the purchaser a whole day at least to make them himself.

Specialisation had its problems, and Adam Smith and Karl Marx both wrote of the danger of mind-destroying social alienation if there is too much specialisation and not enough time for leisure, social and intellectual pursuits.

The satanic mill theory. But both Smith and Marx also identified specialisation and the international trade that would result as a means of peace and development through economic co-operation. Societies that specialise advanced in medicine, public works and living standards.

The whole thrust of civilisation has been to progress and expand freedom, both materially and socially. Throughout history it has fallen to governments to make and enforce the rules that ensure this end. Government is not in contradiction to openness. Sometimes it takes the force of the state to insist on openness. Vested interests will always conspire against the rest of us to protect themselves. It's when they combine to control both the market and the politicians that we have to fear.

Societies where social cohesion functions without the need for rigid or violent enforcement by the state tend to do better. Germany and Japan are examples, both economically and socially. The larger a country's police force, and the more detailed and intrusive its laws, the more expensive the 'transaction costs' of monitoring and enforcing civil agreements. Take as an example the medical system in the United States, where each doctor must pay $100,000 a year just for insurance against litigation. The United States has five times as many lawyers per capita as New Zealand. It is said that in a small American town one lawyer will starve, but two will both make a good living.

The will to co-operate without coercion is the key to success. It's the basis of civil society. Countries, companies and individuals that litigate, sue or blacklist in frustration at the failure of another party to co-operate join in the common failure to resolve a problem.

Plato spoke of an ideal republic where the citizen was so well educated and trained as a citizen 'that no enforcement against him of particular duty, nor system of sanction, would be required, nor anti-civic act, wilful or inadvertent, be committed by him'. Rousseau in *The Social Contract* warned against worship of the state, which he said was not the act of a free citizen but of a subject or slave.

What builds a strong civilised society? The answer is its institutions, customs and culture. That is its social capital. These in turn are based on that fundamental concept of reciprocity: the expectation that your neighbour, competitor, teacher, your daughter's fiancé, the courts, the police and the suppliers of goods you purchase will do the right thing. That they will act in accord with civil and honest behaviour. They will display integrity and honour, based on common values.

Where that social trust is broken, society retreats. When a politician lies to the people by promising no surcharge, no student fees, and no new taxes, he betrays trust and shows by his example that civil order can be broken. The same is true of a police officer who has taken a bribe, a teacher who has given up, or a parent who is more interested in housie than his or her children's education. If the very wealthy appear to pay no tax while the poor battle on, it is seen as immoral and wrong. It destroys social trust and betrays our common values.

It is people's mutual co-operation within the accepted rules that makes for a civilised society. In his book *Making Democracy Work* Robert Putnam writes:

> Compatriots who interact in many social contexts are apt to develop strong norms of acceptable behaviour and to convey their mutual expectations to one another in many reinforcing encounters. These norms are reinforced by the network of relationships that depend on the establishment of a reputation for keeping promises and accepting the norms of the local community regarding behaviour.
>
> Networks of civic engagement facilitate communication and improve the flow of information about the trustworthiness of individuals ... Trust and co-operation depend on reliable information about the past behaviour and present interest of potential partners, while uncertainty reinforces dilemmas of collective action. Thus, other things being equal, the greater the communication (both direct and indirect) among participants, the greater the mutual trust and the easier they will find it to co-operate.

This presupposes the Christian ethic that we are created in God's image; thus, we are all brothers and sisters in the eyes of God. That's the moral force of democracy. We are equal but not the same. Charles Darwin, whose work on evolution challenged the biblical theory of Creation, wrote:

> As man advances in civilisation, small tribes are united into larger communities. The simplest reason should tell each individual that he ought to extend his social instincts and sympathies to all the members of the same nation, though personally unknown to him. This point being once reached, there is only an artificial barrier to prevent his sympathies being extended to the men of all nations and races.[3]

In a more humanist age these 'God-given rights' are called human rights. The age of science eventually eclipsed the age of God and religion as the dominant rational global force. From Christ to the prophet Mohammed, from Darwin through to Marx, the brotherhood of man has been the ultimate goal and sermon.

The Americanisation of our values system, based on the founding fathers' promise that every citizen has a right to 'the pursuit of happiness', is only part of the story. A significant aspect concerns our responsibilities and duty to oneself and the community. Democracy, civil engagement and popular participation are more than the two-minute exercise of ticking a name and a party once every three years. They are about how you live your life.

Open democracy is the most basic component of civil society. It is no historic mistake that democratic states with free markets do better. It is no fluke of nature that democratic trade unions and free institutions are a consistent factor in a nation's economic and social success. It is no accident that the historic changes in Eastern Europe in recent years began with trade unions, from the pivotal role of Solidarity in Poland to the attempted coup in Moscow, which was ended with the threat of a general strike. Free trade unions are a basic component of a democratic economy. It's about checks and balances, not cheques and brutal power.

The President of a new Czechoslovakia, Vaclav Havel, said that political repression in Eastern Europe had robbed those nations of a healthy civic life and worthwhile public institutions:

> Trade unions, democratic involvement and management of our health systems, public ownership of our energy system, are important to our life, our way of doing things. Eastern Europe's problems were not only problems of shortages of private investment, but because public investment and structures, from phones to roads to schools, were in disrepair.

This unique poet/politician, imprisoned by the Marxists, not only saw his country become independent of the Warsaw Pact, but witnessed the country break into two separate nations, the Czech and Slovak republics. Both independent countries now want to join the European Union and NATO.

The West has a better environmental record not only because the market is better than the state, but because democratic civil engagement by the people had demanded it of politicians. The green protest movement plays an important role in a democracy. Public officials and industrial managers in the communist East were free from public pressure and scrutiny. The cruel orphanages of Romania and China could not survive an exposé by the news media of a free society, where the powerful are accountable through free elections.

Co-operation, reciprocity, democracy. What is good for the individual is good for the community; what is good for the nation evolves into a good for the family of nations.

Just as individuals co-operate in all sorts of ways for the wider community good, so must nations. The nation state evolved to resolve problems that individuals, tribes and feuding princes could not. Internationalism has, in turn, grown in significance as the solution to border disputes between nations.

Reciprocal treatment is the basic principle of all the main international forums and agreements: the United Nations and the World Trade Organisation (WTO), the Law of the Sea, the Asia-Pacific Economic Co-operation Forum (APEC), and the European Union (EU).

Today the true patriot and good citizen must also be an internationalist. We serve ourselves best when we serve others. The nation state needs the co-operation of others to progress. International rules and institutions protect and promote individual nations' interests. They enhance independence, which in a modern world is best achieved by interdependence.

The age of empire is over: the age of enlightened internationalism is hopefully nearly upon us. We are now reaching nationalist goals by means of international institutions. I see internationalism as the next step in an evolutionary process that gives voice to a wider democracy and a force for peace and progress.

Democracy thrives on information and the competition of ideas. But politicians are not averse to manipulating language to further their own ends. We were warned in George Orwell's book *1984* of the dangers of 'newspeak' and 'doublespeak': government slogans that said things like 'War is Peace', 'Freedom in Slavery' and 'Ignorance is Strength'. (Iraq's Saddam Hussein must have read Orwell because he recently told his people that if the Americans came back he would give them another thrashing.)

National rights and international rights are fraught with dangers and life will never conform to theories. Nationalism taken to extremes is inevitably perverted to racism. As Sir Arthur Keith said,

> [Hitler] perfected the double standard of in-group morality and out-group ferocity by calling his movement National Socialism. Socialism stood for communitarianism within the tribe, nationalism for its vicious exterior.

When I first read *1984* as a teenager I thought government and big business would be able to control the information age and thus control people. I was wrong. The opposite has happened. The information age, faxes, video cameras and mobile telephones helped the liberation of Eastern Europe by showing the failures of Marxism. The truth will out. It was the faxes, mobile phones and hand-held video cameras that told the world about Tienanmen Square, not the diplomatic community.

The so-called internationalism of Marx set back the post-colonial Third World for two generations. The siren call of Marxism and its anti-imperialist, colonialist message was seductive, given the horror, terror and suffocation of human, political and economic rights under colonial rule.

Yet no single encyclopaedia could store all the treaties, constitutions, bilateral and international agreements that have made the world safer and better over the past decades. There is a staggering collection of conventions and treaties covering everything from air law, postal services, human rights, armed conflict, aliens, refugees, immigration, extradition, governmental co-operation in customs and just about every other government agency, diplomatic law, rights of self-defence, genocide, labour, environmental, rights of indigenous people, commerce, trade, the seabed, adoption, nationality, outer space. It's never-ending. Okay, it's not perfect – it never will be.

But the continuing drive towards that better world is a distinguishing feature of our species. A world without these imperfect mechanisms would be much more dangerous.

Lest the easily excited reach for their pens in the fear that all this prefaces an argument for World Government, let me assure you it does not. A so-called World Government would be unworkable and wrong. No one believes this except the paranoid ultra left or ultra right, who think it is the secret agenda of world leaders. Correspondents tell me the World Court was being organised aboard the royal yacht *Britannia*. A campaign for World Government would force a reaction that would blast apart the progress we have achieved through the evolution of civil and democratic internationalism and the rule of law and treaties.

My argument is that global and regional laws and rules are necessary if we are to save our environment, protect the world's stocks of migratory fish and fowl, establish fair rules for trade and labour, and provide more effective political and economic security. It's imperfect and painfully slow, but through international institutions, examples are steadily building up a treasure of case studies that is producing a common view which will result in more common democratic and peaceful precedents.

With these forms of collective security it is easier to imagine a world with fewer wars. There will always be the Hitlers, Stalins and Saddam Husseins. How far we let them prosper will be the test of robust internationalism.

CHAPTER FOUR

Trade and the New World Economy

If we choose to hide behind walls rather than tear them down, our products will face higher tariffs; our services will be harder to sell; our businesses will find it more difficult to win contracts; our economy will create fewer jobs; and – because we are absent from the bargaining table – we will have no success at all in promoting higher environmental and labour standards.

— United States Secretary of State Madeleine Albright

NOWHERE IS THE DOCTRINE of independence through interdependence more relevant to New Zealand than in the area of trade. I am an internationalist. I come from a political party that has, historically, been internationalist in its foreign policy, but only in the last decade been internationalist in economic policy. If I have contributed anything to New Zealand, and to my party, it has been to lead the charge for this kind of economic internationalism.

Today information is power, thus education is everything. The wealth of nations now, and in the future, will be based not upon their raw resources of cheese, iron, or even oil. It will be based on the capacity of their people to produce, to think, to challenge and to act rapidly and decisively. Information and education are the electricity and power of the new knowledge-based economy.

In the financial markets national boundaries in developed countries, at least, have largely disappeared, as Reserve Bank governor Don Brash pointed out in a recent speech. This fact, together with new technologies, new financial instruments and new funding techniques, means that financial intermediation is increasingly global.

'Fundamental to this trend,' said Dr Brash, 'has been the way in which advances in computer and communications technology have reduced the costs of cross-border transactions by lowering the costs of collecting and analysing data, undertaking transactions, clearing and settling payments and monitoring financial flows.'

The cost of a three-minute telephone call between London and New York has fallen from US$300 (in 1996 dollars) in 1930 to US$1 today, and the cost of computer processing power has been falling by an average of 30 per cent a year in real terms over the past couple of decades.

Fifty million personal computers were sold in 1995, compared with 35 million cars. It is estimated that the speed of data transmissions will increase by a factor of 45 between now and 2005. Such trends, Dr Brash says, allow both the users of financial services and financial institutions themselves to look to global solutions to their financial problems. Funds can now be raised and invested, currencies exchanged and financial risk positions changed around the world at the push of a button.

> Contributing to the globalisation of finance has been the rapid trend towards financial market liberalisation. This has seen country after country freeing up their financial system. In that process, exchange controls (that had been intended to isolate domestic markets from global influences) have been dismantled. In the increasingly integrated global capital market that has resulted, global financial firms with often complex financial and corporate structures have emerged as dominant players. These firms are to be found operating around the globe – relatively low transaction costs and the application of new technologies allow such firms to be active players in whichever of the world's financial markets they want to participate in.

Multinational companies once arrived in a host country like New Zealand and said, 'Give us a monopoly or a share in your tyre industry. Protect us with tariffs and we will give you jobs and tyres.' In the end, because there was no international and little domestic competition, their profits were guaranteed and wages ballooned. It was really a tax on every farmer and widow who had to pay unfair prices for tyres.

The transnational is a different creature. It sources from all over the world – a motor from Germany, design from Japan and marketing from the United States. The world car is born as global strategic alliances between the great car-makers are struck and new great corporations emerge such as the Mercedes/Chrysler and VW/Rolls-Royce mergers.

Of the top 100 economies in the world only 49 are countries – the rest are transnational corporations. The combined sales of the world's top 200 corporations surpass the combined economies of 182 nations – minus the nine largest. These corporations have almost twice the economic power of the poorest 80 per cent of the world's people. They control more than 25 per cent of the world's economic activity. A third of all international trade now takes place within transnationals.

In 1995 an average of US$1.2 trillion flowed through the world's foreign exchange markets each day, according to a survey by the Bank for International Settlements. This figure was 45 per cent higher than in 1992. The bank estimated that the turnover of over-the-counter derivatives on an average day was US$880 billion, 70 per cent of which involved transactions with counterparties in different countries. *Institutional Investor* reported that 'nearly US$150 billion of net new private capital poured into the main Latin American and Asian economies in 1996, almost double the 1995 level'.

There can be no doubt about the role increased trade has had on the economy of individual participant countries. From the early 1970s to the mid-1990s average world GDP growth was around 2 per cent. The prediction is that growth could average 3 to 4 per cent over the next 20 years.

A United Nations world economic and social survey noted that the circle of economic growth had spread to most parts of the world. Of the 95 countries it covers, only 11 failed to increase per capita output in 1996, compared with 24 in 1995. While the ratio of trade growth averaged 1.6 a year for the whole postwar period, it has varied from a low of 1.2 in 1974-84 to a high of 2.8 in 1984-94. Trade now accounts for 20 per cent of world production compared with just 6 per cent four decades ago. And trade is outpacing production; real export growth has averaged more than 6 per cent a year, whereas real output growth has been below 2 per cent.

In the face of this kind of progress, how much sense does protectionism make? As the former Social Democratic Chancellor Helmut Schmidt of Germany put it, 'National strategies are anachronistic in our present-day world.' He pointed out that for small countries like Holland or Luxembourg it is outdated nonsense to even think of a purely national economic policy, a purely national foreign policy or a purely national security policy. Even the super-economies of Japan and the United States cannot by their own national means alone achieve their economic goals, their political goals or even their external security.

The lesson of the last 25 years is that no individual country can any longer successfully prime its economic growth pump. France's Mitterrand discovered this in the 1980s when all he succeeded in doing was flooding his country with imports from Italy and Germany. He eventually reversed his position. Tony Blair's government in Britain is now going through the same restructuring process as the Labour government began in New Zealand. He is called progressive; we were called reactionary. Seems it's wrong to be right too soon.

Peter Drucker argues that 'the world economy is not changing: it has already changed, in its foundations and in its structure, and the change is irreversible'.

Within the last decade or so, two fundamental changes have occurred in the fabric of the world economy:

- In the industrial economy, production has become uncoupled from employment – growth does not always mean more jobs. In fact, in some industries job-shedding is a prerequisite for growth.
- Capital movements rather than trade (in both goods and services) have become the driving force of the world economy.

Drucker says that although capital movements and trade in goods and services have not quite become uncoupled, the link has become loose and, worse, unpredictable. These changes, he argues, are permanent rather than cyclical:

> We may never understand what caused them. The causes of economic change are rarely simple. It may be a long time before economic theorists accept that there have been fundamental changes, and longer still before they adapt their theories to account for them. Above all, they will surely be most reluctant to accept that it is the world economy in control, rather than the macroeconomics of the nation state on which most economic theory will exclusively focus.

The important message for New Zealand is that no nation can hope to survive by ignoring this global reality, unless they want to have Albanian or North Korean standards and styles of living. In Seddon's time, coal was king. In Savage's time it was diesel.[1] Now it is communications, information and education. The cliché of the global village is now a reality.

I saw it illustrated during a visit to Papua New Guinea. A senior public servant showing us around said his father had never met a white man until the age of 50. He, in turn, had been educated at an Australian university, and lived in a village where his son communicated with a penfriend in America via computer and satellite. He smiled and said, 'I have one foot in the stone age and one foot in the space age.'

New Zealand accounts for barely 0.06 per cent of the world's population and our slice of the world's trade is a minuscule 0.27 per cent. Like it or not, the world economy will always drive us; we will never drive it. Understanding and accepting the reality of the global economy is a key first step to shaping our response and lifting our living standards.

More than 60 per cent of New Zealand jobs are related to open investment, trade and tourism. And 70 per cent of our trade is with Asia-Pacific Economic Co-operation members. When I was born, 90 per cent of our exports went to Britain. A larger percentage of New Zealand's economy is based on exports than is the case for Japan, the United States or Germany. South Korea now takes almost as much of our exports as England.

Our living standards – how we eat, our entertainment trends, what we wear, even what we believe – are frequently beyond our control. When Batmania swept New Zealand, it happened because of movies made in the US. The Spice Girls are not Kiwis, but try telling that to your nine-year-old daughter. Fashion shows in Paris help dictate world demand for our wool. Health-food fads in California can help or hinder our export industry. We have to ensure New Zealand is a benefactor rather than a victim of global circumstances.

In order for New Zealand to maintain strong growth it has been estimated that $75-100 billion of new investment will be required over the next five years. It is highly unlikely a flow of new capital in this order could be achieved from onshore sources alone. The alternative to investment is borrowing on international capital markets.

Much suspicion has been focused recently on the OECD's proposed Multilateral Agreement on Investment (MAI). This agreement would lay down rules on investment to match the rules on other forms of trade, based on the principle that all are treated equally. Some New Zealanders apparently find the MAI proposal very threatening. Yet today some one-third of the New Zealand workforce (593,000 individuals) are in jobs within enterprises that are based either directly or indirectly on foreign investment. If tourism were regarded as offshore expenditure, that figure would rise to 800,000 jobs.

Contrary to what some would have you believe, a recent KPMG survey found that 90 per cent of value added by foreign-owned companies remains in New Zealand. Only 10 per cent of profits are remitted offshore. The KPMG survey found that only 0.25 per cent of staff in foreign-owned companies are non-New Zealanders. Two-thirds of the CEOs of these companies are New Zealanders. Furthermore, foreign-owned companies pay their employees an average 28 per cent above the New Zealand average wage.

Seven of the top 10 current sources of foreign investment are OECD members, the survey found. In order of importance to New Zealand they are: the US, Australia, Britain, Canada, Switzerland, Japan and Germany. Hong Kong and Singapore are also in the top 10.

International agreements such as the MAI do not pose a threat to any country's sovereign status unless they let it. The MAI would not change any domestic legislation here in New Zealand. Our own Overseas Investment Commission would still have control over what money was invested here, and we would have reservations on the Treaty of Waitangi. The MAI would no more supersede the treaty than it would the US Constitution. Nothing would change, so why has the New Zealand government backed down and split over it?

Fear, a by-election and a well-organised, well-targeted public campaign against investment, that's why. A deranged group of Maori activists, the usual suspects, marched across the Auckland Harbour Bridge in April of this year, disrupting the busiest road in the country, protesting against an international investment agreement that, far from weakening the Treaty of Waitangi, would enshrine it for the first time in international law.

The MAI debate in New Zealand speaks of failure at all levels, including that of the media, who find it easier to discuss personalities and motives and politics than to address the issues that confront our people. The lack of intelligent debate on this issue, the lack of leadership, information and direction is creating a democratic deficit. People need to know what's in it for them. What's it about? It's about jobs, a safer, cleaner environment, and a more secure, stable, global political economic and social environment.

The MAI was designed to protect and encourage foreign investment because it is such investment that has helped fuel global economic growth and the increasing globalisation of wealth. After the Second World War the United States was literally the only wealthy nation; now Europe, North Asia and South East Asia can all genuinely be described as wealthy regions, with Latin America and East Asia fast becoming economic powerhouses as well, despite their short-term problems. Foreign investment is the instrument of this economic success, and international agreements liberalising trade and investment have played key roles: the GATT, APEC, ASEAN, NAFTA, MERCOSUR, CER.

The postwar Marshall Plan (from which the OECD grew) formed the basis of global reconstruction and saved us from the depression and violence that arose from the 1914-18 Great War settlement. Even some Labour MPs opposed the Marshall Plan, calling it the Martial Plan. Yet it was the most generous act of victorious nations in world history; unlike the 'Peace Treaty' of 1919 at Versailles, which set the stage for another world war.

The loudest critics of the MAI use arguments that are based on misguided patriotism, mistrust of foreigners, a touch of xenophobia, and are conveyed in simplistic messages with little reference to objective fact. Use of emotive terms like 'foreign ownership' frightens people.

New Zealanders get excited when an Australian company wants to open a factory in New Zealand, and so they should because it delivers jobs to communities that can't provide them themselves. Then, if the company wants to leave, the same politicians who campaigned against the initial 'foreign' investment demand that the government subsidise (through tariffs) the investor to keep the factory open. It is the height of political hypocrisy and intellectual dishonesty. The same MPs who stand outside car factories complaining about job losses stand up in Parliament and oppose foreign investment. It's a poisoned political carrot they offer.

Another poorly understood effect of globalisation of world markets is that it stands to benefit poorer, developing nations as well as the front-line economic states. As US Secretary of State Madeleine Albright has said:

> Beggar thy neighbour doesn't work; prosper with thy neighbour does. Second, the driving force behind economic growth is openness: open markets, open investment, open communications and open trade. This is fundamental. Protectionism is an economic poison pill. We cannot expect to gain access to new markets elsewhere if we put a padlock on our own.
>
> Third, when we make progress on the international economic front, we make progress on all fronts. A world that is busy growing will be less prone to conflict and more likely to co-operate. Nations that have embraced economic reform are more likely to move ahead with political reform. And as history informs us, prosperity is a parent to peace.

Charlene Barshefsky, US Trade Representative, summed up trade ministers' mission as not simply to increase the volume of global commerce, but to improve the quality of people's lives. Otherwise why do it?

The World Health Organisation Report 1998, entitled *Life in the 21st Century – A Vision for All*, reports that:

> For example, food supply has more than doubled in the past 40 years, much faster than population growth. Per capita GDP in real terms has risen by at least 2.5 times in the past 50 years. Adult literacy rates have increased by more than 50 per cent since 1970. The proportion of children at school has risen while the proportion of people chronically undernourished has fallen.

Says Madeleine Albright:

> The evidence is clear that globalisation is not lowering standards around the world, it is raising them. Open economies are more likely to lift people

out of poverty than economies that are stagnant and closed. It is no accident that as East Asian nations have reformed their economies during the last quarter century, the percentage of their citizens who are poor has plummeted, and large, educated middle classes have emerged. This, in turn, has created new pressures for decent wages, environmental protection and greater democracy.

The US economy has never been stronger, with low inflation, low unemployment, sustained growth. But even with this success Congress is reluctant to advance free trade.

Ross Perot, the leading US anti-free trade campaigner, is, if nothing else, a gifted misuser of the English language. While waging his highly idiosyncratic – but highly effective – populist campaign against NAFTA and the loss of American jobs he claimed free trade would cause, he coined the now famous phrase 'giant sucking sound' to describe the effect of jobs disappearing across the Tex/Mex border.

Like most of the critics of trade liberalisation before him, Perot's argument was based on a simple observation: it costs far less to hire a Mexican worker than an American worker. Thus, with free access back into the US market, so Perot argued, huge numbers of US labour-intensive firms would relocate to the source of cheap labour. The same argument was used by the old left in New Zealand about CER and the GATT.

The fundamental fallacy behind this argument is well known. The fallacy is, of course, to look at nominal wage rates and nothing else. In reality, wage rates cannot be divorced from other costs of production and other issues that influence the decisions of companies on where to locate their businesses. In particular, this now ancient economic fallacy ignores the issue of labour productivity.

Let's go beyond Ross Perot's striking metaphor to examine the specific case of job losses in the US as a result of NAFTA. There are numerous studies but the one I find most revealing is a study by the US General Accounting Office (GAO).[2]

As part of the political price for getting NAFTA through the US Congress, a special adjustment assistance fund was set up to help American workers who considered they had been displaced by free trade with Mexico and Canada. Not a bad idea in itself in a country that can afford it. But after four years of operation a cumulative total of 150,000 Americans had filed for benefits under this programme.

Let me now admit a secret. I was, in an earlier stage of my life, a unionist and later a social worker when much of my time was spent maximising the opportunities the system provided. On the basis of this experience I can assure you that if there was a halfway plausible argument any union delegate (or individual worker) could mount to get financial assistance from the government there is not a delegate in the US who would not give it a go. For the cost of a postage stamp?

In reality, there is not the slightest possibility that *all* these 150,000 jobs disappeared as a result of free trade with Mexico and Canada. If one were to examine in detail the companies concerned, one would unquestionably find all sorts of problems to do with their firms' competitiveness, the impact of new technology, the effectiveness of their marketing and distribution strategy – plus a hundred other potential causes of job losses.

Further, the statistic of 150,000 'displaced by free trade' takes no account of US jobs created (or maintained) through US exports to Mexico. This is no small issue. Without the financial support of the IMF rescue package, and NAFTA to keep the US market open for Mexican exports, import demand for US goods in Mexico after its currency crisis would have plummetted and, at the margin, tens of thousands of US workers dependent on trade with Mexico would have lost their jobs.

On this occasion, however, I invite readers to ignore all these more sophisticated (but relevant) facts and make an obviously erroneous assumption: that indeed every single one of those 150,000 jobs for which government subsidies were claimed was in fact lost as a result of free trade. Now, I feel strongly for these workers. But as the source of this GAO study observed, the US economy, over the same four-year period, *created 150,000 new jobs approximately every three weeks.*

I have no doubt that trade liberalisation results in some degree of job displacement. I have enormous sympathy for those subject to that displacement, just as I have enormous sympathy for anyone displaced for any reason. However, equally I have no doubt that overall, trade liberalisation around the world creates jobs, raises income levels and gives workers caught in poverty traps in developing countries the means to extricate themselves in the long term.

It is a tragedy that what I am saying is controversial. A poll taken in late 1997 by *Business Week* found that some 56 per cent of Americans believed that 'expanded trade leads to a decrease in the number of jobs'.[3] In fact, international trade is a huge worldwide job-creating machine and the US economy is about the most successful cog in that machine. Over the 20-year period to 1990, average growth in employment in the US was about four times that in the EU. Nor is it true that these new jobs, as it is often argued, are all low-paid 'McJobs' – flipping burgers in fast-food outlets. More that 75 per cent of the new jobs created paid higher-than-average US wages.[4]

World Trade Organisation Director General Renato Ruggiero exposed this fraudulent argument in a recent speech:

> Over the past 10 to 15 years, when developing countries have more and more embraced trade liberalising policies, there have been signs that the tide is turning. The share of developing countries in world trade overall has increased from 20 to 25 per cent. For the manufactured sector it has doubled from 10 to 20 per cent, and on current trends could exceed 50 per cent by the year 2020. Furthermore, in this same period of time, 10 developing countries with a combined population of 1.5 billion people have doubled their income per head.
>
> And while the gap between countries is in some cases widening, it is also true that from 1990 to 1996, developing countries recorded an average growth of 5.4 per cent, three times more than advanced economies. In this same period of time, exports from the industrialised countries to the developing countries grew each year by an average of 10.1 per cent, while exports from developing countries to the industrialised world grew an average of 7.3 per cent. This is the virtuous circle of globalisation.[9]

I have fought for economic opening, not only because I believe it is good for New Zealand, but because I believe it is the best way of assisting poor and developing countries. Opponents of an open economic strategy claim it exploits the poor of developing countries, as well as the poor of New Zealand. But we know that the people of the Philippines don't want handouts: they want access for their products. What is true for our kiwifruit, sheepmeat and fish is equally true for sugar of the Philippines, the rice of Thailand and the manufactured products of Malaysia.

One dollar's worth of transfer to developing countries through higher agricultural prices is equivalent to between $2.20 and $14 in foreign aid. A dollar of well-spent aid can raise incomes by between $1.20 and $2. Compare this with the increase in income of between $4.50 and $27.30 made possible by every dollar transferred to developing countries (excluding the oil exporters) through an increase in world agricultural prices. Julius Nyerere, former president of Tanzania, put it very well: 'It is as true for a nation as it is for a village shopkeeper that the poverty of your potential customers is a limitation upon your own affluence.'

New Zealand was in the vanguard of the launching of the GATT Uruguay Round. We did it through self-interest, but we also did it through principle. Far from developing countries being exploited through such processes, the opposite is true. It is developing countries with their tropical products and manufacturing skills that have the most to gain. In a global economy in an interlocked world the truth is that everybody's well-being, wealth and security is based on the relative success of its trading partners.

Investment agreements like the MAI will be of the greatest long-term benefit to developing nations. In fact the negotiation of a multilateral investment agreement should never have been attempted in the OECD – an organisation of developing countries. It is like one hand clapping. The intellectual work should have been done in the OECD but the negotiation should have awaited the start of a multilateral negotiating round of the WTO. It should have started with developing countries on board from the very start. This will now be much harder to achieve because the wrong judgment call was made in the first instance. But it must still be on the agenda in a balanced way.

Capital injections are desperately needed in many parts of the developing world. Due to the unstable nature of many of the governments in such countries, foreign investors have been reluctant to commit to long-term development and projects requiring infrastructure investment.

Indeed, the Asian economic crisis and the problems in Russia might have been avoided if a transparent regime on open investment had existed in place of cosy crony capitalism and the moral hazard created by laws from which the powerful can benefit.

Those who argue that the WTO denies the sovereignty of nations are plain wrong. The opposite is the truth. Rules protect sovereignty. The reality is that New Zealand's sovereignty has been enhanced by opening up our economy. As Business Roundtable executive director Roger Kerr has said, in 1984 New Zealand was sinking into debt to the rest of the world:

> Today, after reducing external barriers and signing up to agreements such as CER, the GATT Uruguay Round and APEC, the government has repaid all its net foreign currency debt and is running fiscal surpluses. We entered those agreements because they had the potential to make us wealthier and more secure – with more sovereignty over our destiny.

Overseas Trade Minister Lockwood Smith has estimated that New Zealand could gain hundreds of millions of dollars a year from APEC work on the liberalisation of fish and forest products. The deal signed late in 1997, he said, means more jobs and a stronger economy as trade barriers in these and another seven sectors are phased out.

Over the past two decades open economies grew by an average of 4.5 per cent while other economies grew by an average of 0.7 per cent. What has fuelled this growth? Liberalisation of markets for their goods, and a trebling of foreign direct investment.

We are learning. The 1987 sharemarket crash was greater and deeper than the Wall Street crash of the 1920s. But the world did not plunge into a lasting depression. Leaders' nerves held: there wasn't the orgy of protectionism and tariff increases that accompanied the 1920s crash. So far, so good.

The turmoil that struck Asian markets in late 1997, causing some currencies and sharemarkets to plummet by up to 50 per cent, had been predicted for several years. In 1994 China, the engine-room of Asian growth, halved the value of its currency. This hurt Asian competitors, but their crisis was delayed because currencies were pegged to the United States dollar, which was falling. The time of reckoning for overheated economies such as those of Indonesia, Thailand, Malaysia and South Korea arrived with a bang.

What happened? Cheap money poured into unproductive, speculative property markets. Governments invested money they did not have into infrastructural projects that were neither productive nor competitive, and gave poor returns: an Asian version of New Zealand's Think Big projects of the early 1980s. This, on top of bad bankruptcy laws, murky industry support programmes, political and economic nepotism and corruption, created the most dangerous economic situation since the crash of 1987 and the Great Depression of the 1930s.

The assistance packages offered by the International Monetary Fund are a bitter pill as they require radical reform by the recipient nations. But for the donor nations, including New Zealand, such aid amounts to economic peace-keeping. Economic failure somewhere begets social dislocation, which threatens stability, thus everyone's security.

New Zealand's $60 million towards the relief package was a cheap investment. Australia put up $3 billion. Asia 2000 Foundation chairman Philip Burdon pointed out that signing New Zealand up to a modest share in the rescue package cost us very little, with the prospect of considerable long-term gain in goodwill throughout the region. Rather than turning away from Asia, he said, we needed to take a long-term view: 'People in Asia tend to place a premium on stability in relationships. They will take careful note of those who stood by them in difficult times.'

Mexico was bailed out a few years ago by a US-led IMF package. That economy is now on track and is a useful and growing participant in the global economy. The lessons from history are clear. The IMF's medicine is tough. Who likes the doctor who tells you to lose weight and change your diet? But most governments have learnt that you cannot spend or borrow your way to prosperity. In fact the 'bail-out' of Mexico did not cost the US taxpayer one cent; all the money the US has given to the IMF since the fund's inception has been paid back not only in full, but with interest.

Alas, it usually takes a crisis like 1984 in New Zealand or the present Asian economic problems to make governments face the iron reality of economic truth. But the message to these governments is clear. Don't give cronies privileged positions in industry, or handouts. Closed economies, protectionism and subsidies become an open chequebook for the powerful and their friends. They breed inefficiencies and corruption and the powerful never surrender their privileges without a fight.

That was why it was so encouraging to see most Asian leaders courageously facing up to the reality. They have not resorted to heavy protectionism. Mind you, with their currencies so low there's little need. The international community faces several tests in the next two or three years. For the Asian countries, among the many challenges is a simple macroeconomic one: can they convert these huge *nominal* devaluations into *real* devaluations? Can they at least in large part contain the huge inflationary impact of these extraordinary currency realignments?

By itself, a 50 per cent devaluation does not translate (except momentarily) into a 50 per cent increase in competitiveness. New Zealand's own experience tells us this. We were a habitual user of exchange rate devaluations in the 1960s and 70s in a vain attempt to increase the competitiveness of our exporters and import-competing sector. Our problem, however, was that having made a large devaluation, we could never hold on to the temporary increase in competitiveness. We simply did not have the right framework in place, the right attitude, or sufficient commitment to making the adjustments required.

Can the Asian countries in the 1990s do better? At best, their ability to hold on to the gains of the huge currency devaluations is a very open question. It is not clear that they have, in the current climate, the macroeconomic setting in place, or sufficient commitment to microeconomic reform, to hold inflation at bay. They deserve all the support they can get. They will have to increase their exports and Western countries will, in large part, have to absorb that increase.

This will no doubt meet an upsurge in protectionist pressure in Western countries. The US cannot, politically, sustain being the world's market of last resort. That is why Japan is so important as it wrestles to increase domestic purchasing. In the next two or three years we may rediscover the underlying reason for the GATT/WTO system: it puts a floor under protectionism by way of what the technicians call 'Gatt bindings', i.e. international legal commitments not to increase protection. I suspect the era ahead will put some of these commitments very much to the test.

Perhaps the best thing to come out of the Asian crisis is that the model of cosy crony capitalism has been discredited in Chinese eyes and they now look more to the US model than to their near neighbours.

Increased equality and improved human rights will also flow from the liberalising of markets. It makes no sense to refuse to utilise the skills of a future engineer or doctor because they come from the wrong side of town, or are of the wrong colour, race or faith.

The Second World War kicked this process along by bringing women into the workforce. Previously this had been resisted by traditional unions and managers. How stupid is it to run an economy by automatically ruling out the skills of half the workforce because of their gender? Albert Speer, the Nazi Minister in charge of wartime production, claimed after the war that if Hitler had not had a racist fixation on the pure Aryan woman, whose role was to give birth to and raise the master race and who therefore could not possibly work in factories, he would not have needed to use inefficient slave labour to such an extent.

Germany could conceivably have won the war if the full human capital of the country had been utilised. Inequality, racism and religious intolerance are the stuff of closed economies and minds. A more open market and society naturally drifts towards better utilisation of human capital and human rights.

I touched earlier on the issue of the tyranny of location. I wrote a booklet nearly 20 years ago called *On Balance*, in which I suggested that in the future more work would be sourced away from factories to smaller businesses and to people working from home. Telecommuters. Your accountant may now be based in Fiji. If you lose your Visa card, the help-phone line works out of Singapore.

Trade unions in New Zealand were offended and accused me of advocating piecework and poorer conditions. Alas, sometimes this is the effect, but not always. There are now more people in business in the United States than union members. Some 30 million Americans now work alone. In the cyber-industry of the future more and more people will avoid the pain, hassle and tension of going to work if they can. Faxes and email mean much work can be done at home. This has liberated rather than imprisoned many women in successful economies, who can rear children and work their own hours.

Corporations are 'downsizing', sending workers home. A successful US advertising company, Chiat/Day, is abolishing much of its head office, out-sourcing its employees and subcontractors, who work together through the Internet and, when they need to get together, meet in hotels.

I do my best work from home: why go to Wellington? Distance is not miles any more, it's time. Somehow it doesn't seem like work when you are in your old gear, minus shoes and a tie. In the new knowledge-based economy, who will want to travel to work in Los Angeles or Tokyo or London? This trend will accelerate. Remember Moore's law. Intel co-founder Gordon Moore predicted that the number of transistors on a microchip would double every 18 months.

The new economy is an exciting place. The changes it heralds can be seen as presenting a wonderful opportunity or an almighty threat, depending on how we approach them.

George J. Stigler, 1982 Nobel Laureate, was correct when he said of open and competitive markets:

> The competitive industry is not one for lazy or confused or inefficient men: they will watch their customers vanish, their best employees migrate, their assets dissipate. It's a splendid place for men of force: it rewards both hard work and genius and it rewards on a fine and generous scale.

But let's not idealise these opportunities. There will always be a need for social insurance, environmental rules and measures to promote the disadvantaged. To stand up for those who can't make it, to remember the everyday courage of the deserted, the disabled, those who are sick and left out. The measure of civilisation is also about how high we can inch up society's safety-net. An open market without a conscience or compassion is like a truck without a driver. It can accelerate the trend for the rich to become even richer and the poor to become ever more desperate.

If you're still in doubt about the need for change, consider these facts, which will test the tolerance of the people and policymakers. The World Health Organisation Report 1998 predicts that by the Year 2000:

- Worldwide life expectancy, currently 68 years, will reach 73 years – a 50 per cent improvement on the 1955 average of only 48 years.
- The global population, about 5.8 billion now, will increase to about 8 billion. Every day in 1997, about 365,000 babies were born, and about 140,000 people died, giving a natural increase of about 220,000 people a day.
- The number of people aged over 65 will have risen from 390 million in 1997 to 800 million – from 6.6 per cent of the total population to 10 per cent.
- The proportion of young people under 20 years will have fallen from 40 per cent in 1997 to 32 per cent of the total population, despite reaching 2.6 billion – an actual increase of 252 million.
- Even in wealthy countries, most old and frail people cannot meet more than a small fraction of the costs of the health care they need. In the coming decades, few countries will be able to provide specialised care for their large population of aged individuals.
- In 1997 there were 10 million deaths among children under five – 97 per cent of them in the developing world, and most of them due to infectious diseases such as pneumonia and diarrhoea, combined with malnutrition.
- Most of these under-five deaths are preventable. At least 2 million a year could be prevented by existing vaccines.
- One of the biggest hazards to children in the 21st century will be the continuing spread of HIV/Aids. In 1997, 590,000 children aged under 15 became infected with HIV. The disease could reverse some of the major gains achieved in child health over the past 50 years.
- About 1.8 million adults died of Aids in 1997 and the annual death toll is likely to rise.
- More than 50 per cent of pregnant women in the developing world are anaemic.
- About 585,000 women die each year of pregnancy-related causes. Where women have many pregnancies the risk of related death over the course of their lifetime is compounded. While the risk in Europe is one in 1400, in Asia it is one in 65, and in Africa one in 16.

So what do all these figures mean? They mean New Zealand's problems are not unique. Population changes, distribution of wealth and opportunity, work-for-the-dole schemes are on the agenda of every advanced economy. Where do we get the money to pay for our dreams?

Not by building Berlin Walls around the problem, but by international engagement and smart leadership to take advantage of the new age.

CHAPTER FIVE

Our International Structures: A Process of Democratic Evolution

If there is technological advance without social advance, there is, automatically, an increase in human misery, in impoverishment. – Michael Harrington

I'VE ALWAYS SEEN democratic internationalism as the highest form of civilised behaviour. The rule of law, not force. Our species has evolved from tribe to state and is now evolving to save and advance itself by new forms of international co-operation at every level.

Internationalism's purpose ought to be to strengthen, protect and progress the rights of peoples and the nation state, not to replace it.

Malcolm N. Shaw in his magisterial textbook *International Law* concluded with this warning:

> There is a careful balance to be maintained, between inferring necessary powers for the fulfilment of the state's purpose of the organisation and assimilating organisations with states in their possession of wide powers in the context of the international personality.

Shaw is right. No nation will or should willingly surrender its power. Most things are best managed democratically at a local level. Capitals are already too distant from their owners, the people. Internationalism without consent and approval will cause a reaction, revulsion and revolt that will undo the virtues of co-operation.

But there has been a failure at the highest political level to explain and sell the peaceful and democratic virtues and functions of international organisations and arrangements, such as APEC, the World Trade Organisation and the Multilateral Agreement on Investment (MAI), and the benefits they can bring to New Zealand, developing countries and world growth and stability.

For some reason the UN and the ILO are seen as noble but their sister structures, the WTO, IMF and World Bank, as sinister. This is a hangover from the Cold War, when the communists saw them as instruments of capitalism and a threat to Marxist influence. Western Europe was reborn postwar because of the Marshall Plan, but the Marxist masters in Moscow refused to let Eastern Europe avail itself of funds and ideas. Thus Hungary and Czecho-slovakia, whose industries were the equal of France and Britain's before the war, by the 1950s lagged behind the West.

As Senator Daniel Patrick Moynihan pointed out in his book *On the Law of Nations*:

> The point is that international law is not higher law or better law; it is *existing* law. It is not a law that eschews force; such a view is alien to the very idea of law. Often as not it is the law of the victor, but it is law withal and does evolve. There was little that could be called human rights law in Dr Johnson's time; there is much today.

In 1910, on the occasion of accepting his Nobel Peace Prize, US President Theodore Roosevelt shared a grand vision:

> … it would be a masterstroke if those great powers honestly bent on peace would form a League of Peace, not only to keep the peace among themselves, but to prevent, by force if necessary, its being broken by others. The supreme difficulty in connection with developing the peace work of The Hague arises from the lack of any executive power, of any police power to enforce the decrees of the court.
>
> In any community of any size the authority of the courts rests upon actual or potential force; on the existence of a police, or on the knowledge that the able-bodied men of the country are both ready and willing to see that the decrees of judicial and legislative bodies are put into effect …
>
> So it is with nations. Each nation must keep well prepared to defend itself until the establishment of some form of international police power, competent and willing to prevent violence between nations. As things are now, such power to command peace throughout the world could best be assured by some combination between great nations which sincerely desire peace and have no thought themselves of committing aggressions.

As individuals, tribes and nations we live by violence, or by law. The weak and modest need the protection of law more than the mighty, but the mighty also need peace, law, and a clean planet. Coalitions of the smaller players have frequently brought down the mighty throughout history. That's the basis of collective security.

If we accept that civilisation can be measured by the growth of civil society and respect and reciprocity between tribes and nations, a few minutes' thought on how international law evolved is worthwhile. Two thousand years before the birth of Christ the city-state ruler of Umma and Lagash in Mesopotamia carved out on a stone block the defining boundaries that were under dispute.

One thousand years later, Egyptian Pharaoh Rameses II and the King of the Hittites signed a 'paper' for a defence agreement, which acknowledged respect for one another's territories. The Old Testament prophet Isaiah stated that 'sworn agreements, even when made with the enemy, must be preserved'.

International trade and commerce created the need for international law centuries ago to handle disputes, for example to guarantee safe passage to merchant shipping in the high seas. In the past 20 years the law of the sea has been developed to handle ownership questions over the 200-mile economic zone. Early treaties, customs and conventions establishing the integrity of embassies, and asylum for political refugees, are not new to the last two centuries. Such moves represent the early evolution towards international civil society. Without such rules, there would be international anarchy. Even after the bombing of Pearl Harbour, embassies quietly packed and went home. No hostages were taken. Almost civilised?

The Congress of Vienna of 1815, after the Napoleonic Wars, represented the first systematic attempt to regulate at an international level major political differences. For 100 years it institutionalised the balance of power and became a semi-formal international order.

The First World War changed everything. European empires and ideologies had ruled the world but the Great War undermined the foundations of European civilisation. (Incidentally, Mahatma Gandhi, when asked what he thought of European civilisation, said: 'It would be good – when they get one.' Chou En-Lai's response to the same question was: 'It's too early to tell.')

Postwar the 1919 Peace Treaty established the League of Nations because US President Woodrow Wilson, joined by the new liberal and left internationalists, wanted a 'new world'. Alas, the league was undermined by reactionary, fascist and communist disregard for its principles, and became merely a European instrument. The UN arose to take its place in 1945.

President Wilson's 'rights of nations' were based on four main points:

- There must never again be a foot of ground acquired by conquest.
- It must be recognised in fact that the small nations are on an equality of rights with the great nations.
- Ammunition must be manufactured by governments and not by private individuals.
- There must be some sort of an association of nations wherein all shall guarantee the territorial integrity of each.

Although self-determination became, as Winston Churchill said, 'rightly forever connected with the name President Wilson', it was neither new nor original. But Wilson provided an intellectual vision and passion for other generations and leaders, such as F.D. Roosevelt, to build on. Wilson died a disappointed man, despairing of his own Senate's rejection of his visions. Indeed, it's said that when a visitor whispered to him on his deathbed that the Senate was praying for him he replied, 'But which way, and for what result are they praying?'

We are all neo-Wilsonians now, frequently disappointed when our great agencies fail or when people stubbornly cling to tribal hatred, racism and violence.

During the Second World War the Allied leaders met, not only to discuss winning the war, but to plan for a brave new world after victory. It was a time of grand vision, with sweeping and splendid plans to ban war and want, and to harness the willpower of the people to wage peace as successfully as they were waging war. They knew the origins of the war had been sowed by the vicious reparations of the treaty in 1919, the collapse of the world trading system and the Great Depression, exacerbated by a prolonged outbreak of tariffs and protectionism – Japanese exports halved in a year. These failures gave rise to the twin tyrannies of our age: fascism and Marxism.

In the New Hampshire village of Bretton Woods, great and bold minds met to prepare practical plans to meet the grand designs of their leaders. From these and similar meetings evolved the United Nations, the General Agreement on Tariffs and Trade (later to evolve into the World Trade Organisation), the International Monetary Fund and the World Bank.

In the main, the last 50 years have been an unprecedented time of undeclared war, imperfect peace, growth and uneven prosperity. The institutions born of international postwar solidarity have generally held firm. A world without them would be unthinkable, dangerous and unstable.

The UN is not perfect. It is a stage and should never be expected to function as a pure democracy. If it were to use the system of one nation one vote, Luxembourg would have the same power as Russia, and Nauru the same vote as Brazil. But if voting were to be by population, China and India would outvote the rest of the world every time. That stretches even my battle-scarred idealism. The General Assembly does function as a democracy but the Security Council holds an ace card.

However, the new Security Council ought to reflect contemporary realities, not realities frozen in postwar 1946. Japan and Germany today ought to have political power commensurate with their economic power and the great emerging countries such as India and Brazil better representation, as should Africa. That would start to give the UN more credibility.

Another bugbear for the UN is funding. One of the UN's more high-profile roles of late has been to supply peacekeepers to various troubled parts of the globe, notably the former Yugoslavia. The United Nations does not have an army in the traditional sense of the word. But it can call upon 'armies' of lightly armed peacekeepers in their distinctive blue helmets or berets, whose strongest weapon is their impartiality.

Being impartial can still be a dangerous business. More than 1400 peacekeepers have lost their lives while serving in the 42 UN operations since 1945. Peacekeeping is also an expensive business in dollar terms. The annual bill for personnel and equipment in 1995, at the height of the operation in the former Yugoslavia, was US$2.8 billion. Yet for every dollar that all governments spent on military activities in 1995, less than half a cent went into UN peacekeeping.

Peacekeepers have been handed daunting tasks by the UN Security Council but have not always been given the means to carry them out. In 1994 the Secretary General told the Security Council that peacekeeping commanders would need 35,000 troops to deter attacks on the 'safe areas' created in Bosnia and Herzegovina. Member states authorised just 7600 and took a year to provide them.

Faced with genocide in Rwanda in the same year, the Security Council unanimously decided that 5500 peacekeepers were urgently needed. But it took nearly six months for states to provide the troops, even though 19 governments had pledged to keep more than 30,000 troops on standby for the UN. This became a shameful fiasco, with only President Clinton publicly apologising for the failure of the civilised world to take action.

There is an obligation on member states to pay their share towards peacekeeping, but in September 1996 the outstanding debt had topped US$2 billion. Of the five permanent members of the Security Council, all but France owed varying amounts. The United States was the largest debtor, owing more than US$1 billion, costly to its credibility and moral authority.

There are basic contradictions in the UN charter and practice but that's hardly surprising, and is not evil. The world is full of contradictions, and they change from day to day.

The reality is that in the late 1990s the UN and its sister institutions no longer reflect the needs of the new global economy. They need reform and cohesion. When they were established, Japan and Germany were shattered by war. Politicians still thought in terms of national economies and food security. Jet transport was barely invented. There were no faxes, satellites or Internet. It just was not possible to live in New Zealand and work in Wall Street, New York or Sydney as some 'global' New Zealanders and enterprises now do.

But imperfect as they are, such institutions are needed to give legal life to globalisation. What's lacking is cohesion between these great institutions.

What's also lacking is public understanding, which would build support for them. Parliaments, peoples and pressure groups around the world talk of faceless bureaucrats in Geneva, or at the UN, IMF and WTO. In reality, these organisations are the servants of governments represented by ambassadors or directors, answerable in various ways to their governments, who in turn are accountable to their taxpayers. The only powers they have are powers given to them by sovereign governments.

There has to be more transparency, openness and accountability. Diplomacy is frequently best done in secret, but the demands of the 1990s, with the death of the Cold War and the explosion of NGOs and the Internet must give new life to the democratic impulse.

Ministers will have to take more control, as will governments and taxpayers, as the impact of globalisation reaches into every facet of domestic life.

It's not all the fault of the great institutions. For example, New Zealand's Foreign Affairs Select Committee is only now going to study and report on the work of APEC and the ILO. All institutions end up having a life of their own; accountability goes both ways. Bureaucracy is difficult to manage domestically, let alone internationally.

Overcoming this democratic deficit at an international level will be the challenge of the new generation of public servants and must be insisted upon by their political masters. It will change the nature of the organisations and improve them, making them more relevant, easier to run and more able to seek support. It's an evolutionary democratic process that's under way and it will provide for a better way and world.

As every sage since Aristotle has observed, man is essentially a political animal.

The European Union

The most profound example of how internationalism can work is the European Union.

Twelve of the 15 countries in the EU are now run by social democratic governments. If the SDP wins in Germany that will make 13. A new generation of social democratic leadership has emerged, personified by Tony Blair. They are free and social marketeers. They will give new life to a mature democratic vision of internationalism to match the commercial drive towards globalisation. Isn't that what happened during the industrial age at a national level? The labour/social democratic impulse is to seek collective security through collective engagement – the modern, global approach.

In March 1998 Sir Leon Brittan, vice-president of the European Commission and Commissioner for Foreign Relations, called Europe the new tiger. A European solidarity is emerging. A few years ago I was talking to the children of a Belgian friend and asked them how many medals Belgium had won at the Olympics. 'Europe won the most!' was the excited reply. One poll revealed that when French people were asked who was France's best friend the overwhelming response was Germany.

Europe is now the largest donor of development aid, representing over 50 per cent of all aid from OECD countries.

The European Community has already given way to a larger European Union, and will be an economic and political superpower when these tribes get it together. The EU represents six per cent of the world's population, but accounts for 35 per cent of the total GDP of the OECD countries, and one-third of world trade. The EU accounts for 30 per cent of the world's direct foreign investment.

The new common currency will result in at least a 0.5 per cent increase in GDP, as it provides savings from reduced bureaucracy and the certainty to business provided by having a strong central bank. The Euro, which comes into being in January 1999, will add further dynamism to the European economy as it challenges the US dollar and Japanese yen as a reserve currency. Business people won't have to work through a dozen currencies, predictability will be enshrined in the new central bank, via the Maastricht Treaty. Europe is a clumsy superpower, however, because of its decision-making structure, which quite rightly gives sovereignty to the nation state.

New Zealanders have been brought up on a diet of anti-European sentiment over a generation, a result of the exclusion of New Zealand agricultural products from the developing European market, and the European Common Agricultural Policy. The CAP was born out of the misery and starvation of war, when the issue was food security. This also was the impulse when GATT was formed and New Zealand understood this and raised no objections. Indeed, we had food rationing to free up food for Europe long after food was no longer rationed in Britain. (In so much of what governments do, they start with the best of intentions but then institutions develop lives of their own, way after the critical origins of the policy have been forgotten.)

I support the CAP. I'd rather negotiate one common agricultural policy than lots of individual agricultural policies based on more local imperatives. We have never opposed supporting farmers, but have opposed supporting them through inflating prices. There is an important distinction. Poor families often need support in rural areas, but payments should be made per family or per farm, not per cow or ton of grain. Anyhow, most of the present subsidy doesn't get to the farmer, and what does mainly gets to the middlemen and the richest of the farmers, not the poorest. EU enlargement will put financial and political pressure on all Commission programmes. For example, 30 per cent of Poles live on the land. The need to ensure the new EU is not swamped by economic refugees is central to EU policy-making. But I digress.

Sir Leon explained in his speech:

Let us begin in the first half of the 1980s. ... even as recently as that, Europe was a very different place. Cold War political and economic structures were still in place ... The European Community (as we called it then) consisted of only nine countries.

In those days the European Community was smothering in internal difficulties. We were scrapping over the budget and the Common Agricultural Policy. It was hard to make decisions because votes in our Council of Ministers normally required unanimity of all member states. People talked about eurosclerosis, and they had a point. The glorious postwar years of European growth had petered out.

But in the short period since then, extraordinary things have happened. In 1986 we set out to build the European Single Market, providing for free movement of labour, goods, services and capital between our member states. This gave the European Community a profoundly significant new economic agenda of internal liberalisation. And this was accompanied by an equally radical new departure in decision-making, with the much more widespread use of a qualified majority voting system ...

Three years later the Cold War was suddenly over. The end of the Soviet Union brought new challenges and opportunities for the European Community. At last we were free to set our own agenda, and faced the responsibility of doing just that, in a continent no longer divided.

International agreements will be much easier to broker now that the poison of the old Soviet Union no longer infects international forums.

The Marxist countries with the worst records on human rights somehow managed to capture the imagination of developing countries with their dishonest championship of the Third World and their anti-colonial rhetoric. Stalin talked loudly about the 'nationalities question', which he resolved through genocide. Human rights were just 'bourgeois legalities'.

Communism through Stalin not only wrecked economies for two generations, it also helped undermine the institutions and vehicles set in place to deliver peace and development after the holocaust of the Second World War. The International Labour Organisation (ILO) was derailed because of its resolutions on labelling Zionism as racism, and the World Bank and International Monetary Fund (IMF) have unearned reputations born of the Cold War of being anti-poor, anti-developing countries. The opposite should be the truth. The latter two are guilty on the understandable counts of not being sufficiently sensitive to the environment and enjoying the spectacle of Think Big projects. But so was every government, elected and unelected, at the time. This view of development is changing at a national and international level.

But these days are over. No one believes that any more, except a few deranged misfits on the edges of obscure universities, people who tuck their shirts into their underpants, the remnants of pressure groups and a few geriatrics who claim that Marxism, like Christianity, has not been tried yet. (This debate, of course, only takes place in democracies: not in Iran, China, Iraq or North Korea.)

GATT/WTO
The General Agreement on Tariffs and Trade (GATT), and the World Trade Organisation (WTO), the structure that manages this 23,000-page treaty, are probably the most misunderstood of all the great international institutions. Yet the WTO has far more effect on people's daily lives and living standards than the UN, by providing trading and economic certainty between nations.

Renato Ruggiero, the Director General of the WTO, spelled out its agenda at an international economics conference in Washington earlier this year.

Right from the beginning the mission of the trading system to improve human welfare has been clear. The preamble to the GATT, negotiated in

71

1947, emphasises that trade liberalisation should be conducted with a view to 'raising standards of living, ensuring full employment and a large and steadily growing volume of real income'. For over fifty years the system has fulfilled that mission in a way which has made an immeasurable contribution to creating a more prosperous and stable world.

The multilateral system has contributed to an extraordinary period of growth in world trade and output – growth which in turn generates the economic resources that allow more ambitious and costly environmental and social policies to be put in place ...

More and more countries, especially in the developing world, are being drawn into this system as its relevance and influence expands. While early GATT rounds in the 1950s typically involved some 20 to 30 countries, the Uruguay Round had 123 participants, and today the WTO has 132 members – 80 per cent of which are developing or transition economies.

Far from weakening the integrity of a nation's state and allowing the great multinationals to ravage the world, I believe the GATT and the WTO do the opposite. Each government must sign up and agree to the programmes. The GATT is a contract between nations to treat each other equally, with legal disputes mechanisms to resolve differences. It enhances the sovereignty of small and weak nations. Japan, or the United States, cannot ignore or push around small nations. They cannot do side deals and give each other preferences. For a generation New Zealand trade ministers were humiliated by going to Brussels and Paris, not to negotiate for butter and sheepmeat access to Europe, but to lobby. Now we are independent; our trade rights are guaranteed by international law.

New Zealand Dairy Board chairman Sir Dryden Spring points out that WTO rules

> ... have at last tackled that oldest bogey of the international dairy business – the unbridled use of export subsidies to dispose of surpluses generated by the protection and support policies of the major producers.

Placed in perspective, he says, these developments can be seen as the internationalisation of the dairy foods business:

> ... a process of immense significance which will shape the destiny of the New Zealand dairy industry as we enter the new millennium. It is a future which offers New Zealand's efficient, integrated dairy industry exciting prospects. The products, the brands, the international marketing infrastructure the industry has put in place over many years, position it strongly to prosper in the new environment which is evolving.

Critics of the WTO are often heard to claim that it serves only the interests of the large trading powers. Of course the larger powers exert a stronger influence than the smaller powers. A system that failed to reflect certain realities would not command the confidence of the major powers and would drift quickly into the irrelevance that frankly captures so many other international organisations. But what is remarkable about the WTO is its *legal* character. Here, even the smallest WTO members get real power and protection, provided the legal basis to their case is robust. Chile was able to secure its GATT rights in a head-to-head conflict with the EU over apples in one celebrated case.

Even smaller Costa Rica beat the US through the WTO's binding disputes mechanisms because its case was correct. The 'banana republics' were so called because in the past the US and their multinationals just overthrew the governments of the smaller nations if they didn't toe the line. This was generations ago. Now we have international law.

At a trade ministers' meeting a South American minister told a story of how a group of visiting US congressmen had asked his president why his country, which was 200 years old, had suffered 87 revolutions, while the US, which was also 200 years old, had had only one. 'Perhaps,' the president replied, 'it's because there is no US embassy in Washington.' The US Trade Minister laughed the hardest.

However, the WTO is under pressure, ironically because of its success. Increasingly today because of difficulties resolving issues within the ILO and because many of the Multilateral Agreements on the Environment (MEAs) do not work and the WTO does, there is a worldwide drive by non-governmental organisations (NGOs) to have the WTO adjudicate all these complex issues by linking them to trade.

The danger is that the WTO could become unworkable under the pressure, although it is a very robust institution and the stakes are high. It's curious that some expect 150 nations to be able to agree in that forum on issues they couldn't resolve elsewhere.

There must be a fresh, new harmony between the great institutions, and there will be.

Child Labour

The use of child labour in developing countries has caused worldwide concern, and various international organisations have been active in seeking to eradicate the practice. UNICEF's 1997 State of the World's Children report called on transnational corporations to adopt codes of conduct banning the use of child labour by their suppliers in developing countries.

Among the companies to adopt such codes of conduct so far have been clothing makers Levi-Strauss and Phillips-Van Heusen, athletic footwear makers Nike and Reebok, and retailers Eddie Bauer, The Gap, Nordstrum, J.C. Penney, Sears Roebuck and Co and Wal-Mart. All of these retailers are heavily involved in organising the production of clothing and footwear internationally through outsourcing.

In 1996 the US clothing giant The Gap went even further, by reaching agreement with a coalition of trade union, human rights and religious organisations to establish a system of independent monitoring of the observance of this company's code of conduct by its sub-contractor in El Salvador. Levi's has terms of engagement with its 600 contract manufacturers around the world in which it states that it will not do business with companies that use child or prison labour.

Fifa, soccer's world governing body, has agreed to a code of conduct for manufacturers of soccer balls, after a trade union campaign revealed that souvenir balls for the Euro '96 championship had been produced by child labourers in Pakistan.

New Zealand has yet to follow the more progressive US and the European countries with codes of conduct. Unless business takes the lead, governments will by default.

Yet the drafting of such rules needs to be both precise and culturally broad. How many New Zealand farms would be viable if the children of family members were paid minimum wages? How many apples would be picked or newspapers delivered without the efforts of children in this country? Work is character-building for the young. The family orchard and farm are fundamental to our way of life, and in the life-blood of other societies. We need to ensure treaties and rules reflect fairly local cultures.

Labour Conditions

The issue of wage rates in developing countries is vexed. Wealthy companies often appear keen to take advantage of lower environmental and labour standards in developing countries in order to increase profits, which could be seen as exploitative. On the other hand, why should developing countries not seek to utilise their competitive advantages? Many developing countries see any restrictions as potentially keeping much-needed investment and jobs from their shores.

On the negotiation of the North American Free Trade Agreement (NAFTA), there was and still is strong concern that it would bring downward pressure to bear on wages and working conditions. To accommodate this concern, a 'side' or 'parallel' agreement on labour standards was negotiated. The North American Agreement on Labor Co-operation (NAALC), also commonly known as the NAFTA Side Agreement on Labor, came into force at the same time as NAFTA on 1 January 1994.

The NAALC states that a country's environmental and labour standards must not be downgraded for specific investment bids. It provides for a commitment to uphold existing labour laws in basic areas of workers' rights including freedom of association, the right to collective bargaining and the right to strike, prohibition of forced labour, prohibition of discrimination, protection of migrant workers, health and safety, child protection, and minimum employment standards. In the areas of minimum wages, safety standards and child labour alone, fines of up to $20 million could be levied on countries that allow their companies to gain a competitive advantage by violating local labour laws in these areas.

In response to this dilemma trade ministers at a WTO meeting agreed that nothing should stop nations utilising a labour cost advantage that already exists. Western liberals wince at this. They see the Indian computer programmer receiving only a third of the income of a worker in Houston. However, the Indian computer programmer may be earning 10 times as much as anyone else in his village. Furthermore, his purchasing power with those wages may be commensurately greater by a larger factor. This is what lies behind the concept of PPP – Purchasing Power Parity – best known around the world by the PPP-related measure devised by the *Economist*: the relative cost around the world of purchasing a Big Mac. Now that the OECD and IMF have put a dollar value on democracy, freedom and civil society, and have proved that what should be good in itself also represents a competitive advantage, we will see the World Bank talking good governance, transparency and honest tax laws, and the WTO negotiating open government procurement agreements.

As always, it's a matter of balance, which can best be achieved through greater coherence between the great institutions: the ILO, WTO, IMF and World Bank.

War Crimes and Crimes Against Humanity

One grand idea that sits deadlocked on the desk of UN leaders is the idea for the creation of a permanent war crimes tribunal to cover acts of genocide and crimes against humanity. The UN first studied the concept seriously in 1948, but the Cold War froze progress.

The major powers argue that only the Security Council of the UN (over which they each have a veto) should be able to set in motion an investigation by the tribunal. But why should small nations, without the veto, accept that the great nations could veto proceedings against themselves, or nations historically friendly to them? Great principles lie vulnerable to the grim reality of power politics at the highest possible level.

To be a great nation and to occupy a seat on the Security Council carries great responsibility and greater power. Alas, size is no measure of greatness – ask most men. China and Russia fear the proposal, arguing non-interference in domestic affairs (Tibet and Chechenya). The US, the most generous 'victor' in world history and now the only superpower, has uneasy reservations. It is always American men, women and money that are on the line.

The old left in the West is torn between wanting the US not to have so much power and accepting that most international solutions need US support or approval.

The Russians have even suggested that war crimes tribunals such as the one in the Balkans can actually delay peace because the fearful generals and politicians have no incentive to achieve peace. Peace would see them on trial, so why negotiate a settlement? Unfortunately there is some truth in this.

The South African Truth and Reconciliation Commission, headed by Bishop Tutu, is now heading into difficulties as the search for the truth is uncovering some crimes that once exposed could endanger the stability of that nation.

The formula of 'military' immunity means General Pinochet has a seat in the Senate, unelected for life by a constitution he designed. But sometimes 'peace accords' only come about if the generals are guaranteed immunity for crimes. That's been the South American formula as nations such as Chile and Argentina moved from fascism to a more democratic system. In Argentina a government more confident after a few years of democracy is now reversing the immunity formula and is literally digging up the old bones of the past.

As Minister of Foreign Affairs I began to assemble a project to get together second-tier ANC leadership, under New Zealand sponsorship, to visit countries such as Chile, Vietnam, Hungary and Poland, so they could study and learn the political and economic lesson of how nations moved from command economies and military regimes to more democratic justice and economic systems. Alas, the new National government dropped the idea.

A permanent war crimes tribunal would mean amending the UN charter and would cut into the jurisdiction of the Security Council. By virtue of its existence and mandate it would reduce the sovereignty of the nation state in matters of the conduct of war. But then so does the Geneva Convention. It is hardly surprising that such a complex proposal has not been supported by some of the major powers. But the debate is still very much alive and being negotiated as I write.

Biological Weapons and Terrorism

World governments were silent when Saddam Hussein used chemical weapons against his own people a decade ago, and was armed and encouraged to fight and contain the villain of the time, Iran. Greed, indifference and a larger geo-political view made the West accomplices in a situation that escalated into a global threat.

Existing treaties prohibit biological weapons being held by states but not by individuals. Neither do such sanctions get at the source of manufacturing. Philip Heymann, a former deputy attorney-general in the Clinton administration, and co-author Matthew Meselson, a US professor of biotechnology, see a need for a new treaty that creates international criminal law, applicable to individual offenders.

> Such a treaty would help greatly to deter national leaders from seeking to develop biological weapons, would discourage businesses and nations from assisting them and would keep leading nations from looking the other way in the face of violations.

The new treaty would declare it a crime, punishable by an appropriate international tribunal, for any person to develop, manufacture, threaten to use or use biological weapons. Had such a treaty been in existence in the 1980s, the authors contest, the Western suppliers and advisers on whom Saddam Hussein depended could have been brought to trial.

> Few individuals or corporations would feel comfortable selling dangerous knowledge, ingredients or equipment to a leader who had been branded an international criminal and fugitive. Nations would not be able to look the other way when an indicted international criminal threatened or used chemical or biological weapons on a neighbour or his own citizens.[7]

What's needed is an international criminal court as promoted by former US President Jimmy Carter, because more than ever political violence is perpetrated by rogue groups, not just rogue nations. (The World Court at The Hague handles disputes between nations.)

If the nation state were defended by legal internationalism, blackmailers would find it difficult to threaten small nations. The deterrence of such terrorism is as important as bringing such thugs to justice. Knowing they could be extradited and brought to justice in some cases would change the way they operate.

It would be a difficult procedure to set up. It would require global adherence to a raft of treaties covering extradition, sanctuary, places to manage justice and provide secure prisons, methods of sharing costs and providing sanctions against offender nations and groups.

Only the United Nations offers the global moral reach to bring together such a process. Of course enforcement would be the next headache. But a new international legal architecture is necessary and a few practical carpenters need to be put on the case. No country is safe from international crime or terrorism.

Organised Crime and Drugs

Political crimes and terrorism are in some ways easier to understand and combat than organised crime. Crime is now organised on a global scale.

The world trade in drugs is equal in dollar value to the world's trade in oil. Co-operation between governments, countries and law enforcement agencies is vital to attack this menace at its source as it is destroying a generation of young people and bringing decaying cities to the point of anarchy.

The sheer amount of money involved has corrupted politicians, bureaucrats and the agencies of justice and law enforcement in many countries and cities. Only the blind would pretend that this level of crime can now be beaten, or even contained, at a national level. Bikie gangs who provide the muscle for much of the drug business now even have chapters in such enlightened countries as Denmark and Holland.

Rogue governments, such as that of Burma, and extreme political groups such as the Shining Path in Peru and the IRA fund much of their political ambition from crime and violence. Drugs are a rich vein to mine for the cash to bribe and influence. Drug-running needs discipline and management that relies on devout distribution agents.

The Mafia and Triads began as self-protection unions against feudal power. They have evolved over the generations into criminal conspiracies, their original purpose long since forgotten. They have corrupted governments and civil society. Their strength is their loyalty to 'family' beyond society. They are secret societies beyond national boundaries.

Gangs in New Zealand read white power literature from the US. Their wealth, power and ruthlessness, based on drug distribution, make them a force to be feared. Hell's Angels and the Bandito gangs carry on their wars from Los Angeles to Sweden to Australia, where people have been murdered with sophisticated military weapons. Secret New Zealand police reports made public explain our police's fear of similar gang warfare in New Zealand over drug territories. The world secretary of Hell's Angels International for a while was a New Zealander.

In response to this real threat, all sorts of agencies worldwide are co-operating on all sorts of levels. Law enforcement agencies, immigration, airlines, customs departments, even the security intelligence services that once eyed the KGB are now involved. The international vice must tighten, because the good guys are losing. Try tracing money laundering in the cyber-economy without international agreements.

Copyright and Piracy

Issues of piracy and copyright are also overdue for more attention at an international level.

The film and music awards of the future may well be won by small independent operators working from home. The expensive top-of-the-market technology available in the 1960s and used by the Beatles and Rolling Stones is now available for a few hundred dollars. A news or cinema camera that cost half a million dollars a decade ago now costs a tenth of that.

Technological advances drop prices and create opportunities for small localised TV and radio stations, and ordinary people with nothing other than talent can now have a go. It is now no longer true that the cost of technology allows great corporations to monopolise popular culture.

The arts have always been the most international of industries. Love of music, art, literature and cinema is global in the truest sense of the word. All people are equal in their love of music or appreciation of architecture. Mankind is united in awe as we gaze with wonder at the pyramids or the Great Wall of China, listen to Mozart or view the *Mona Lisa*.

But tougher international laws on copyright are needed to protect the works of artists and the businesses that risk capital to promote them. Piracy is not restricted to history and Spanish galleons. The US administration suggests that piracy of computer work, CDs, videos and so on costs the artists and industry in the US about $60 billion annually.

Similarly, without international rules on copyright, why should investors put up the millions of dollars necessary to find a cure for cancer or Aids? They need to know that the inventions and investment are legally secure.

New Zealand is facing its most difficult trade difference with the US over the New Zealand government's move to allow parallel importing. This means anyone can import any product from anywhere and the local holder of an import licence or franchise loses his or her monopoly. The law was rushed through without proper parliamentary select committee hearings. Hollywood is furious, fearing that pirated products will flow into New Zealand. They are a powerful political influence; in fact the US Trade Representative was moved to warn New Zealand publicly of the implications. This step is unprecedented in our trading relationship.

Corruption and Cosy, Crony Capitalism

For freedom to flourish, both commercial and political, there needs to be the rule of law. The cost of corruption weighs heavy on many economies, slowing progress and stunting democracy. It's not restricted to developing countries and stains political life from Nicaragua to Pakistan, from Spain to Korea, Russia and Italy. Responses to a survey of 3000 firms operating in 59 countries by the World Economic Forum Global Competitive Studies gave graphic evidence that corruption is contagious and is prevalent in mature, democratic developing countries as well as economies in transition.

The cost of such practices is so high that the IMF and World Bank have published learned papers on its impact and how it can be fought. The OECD resolved to criminalise bribery abroad, based in part on the work of an increasingly influential non-governmental organisation, Transparency International.

A major survey of more than 150 top public officials, including representatives of 60 developing countries, ranked public-sector corruption as the most severe impediment to growth, development and the advancement of a more civil society.

Governments have been toppled in major developed and developing countries because of corruption; indeed, corruption and political instability may be two sides of the same coin. I faced it only a few times as Minister of Trade. After one large sale a Middle East minister insisted that he get details of my Swiss bank account. I don't have one. After my position was explained the minister said, 'Tell Mike we offered him his share. We are honest: we always pay.'

Research has shown that when a nation improves its standing on the corruption index as devised by the IMF, say from 6 to 8 (0 is the most corrupt, 10 the least), then that country enjoys a 4 per cent increase in its investment rate and a 0.5 per cent GDP growth rate increase. The same analysis shows that such a country will typically raise its spending on education by 0.5 per cent. This is a most significant statistic, given the link between education standards and living standards.

More and more, public and private aid and investment packages are being linked to the adoption of 'good governance' programmes by the recipient states. Such loans frequently involve a commitment to the eradication of corruption and more democracy.

This is not a new form of colonialism or imperialism, as has been suggested by some. The local bank manager wants to see good business practices in action before he hands out money. Taxpayers who have to fund these 'rescue' packages have grown weary of seeing their money wasted or propping up wealthy elites. Just as the taxpayer is demanding more accountability at home for expenditure, they correctly insist on more prudent practices abroad. And why not? After all, it's their money and much of the commercial bank borrowing and lending comes from workers' savings and retirement funds.

A corruption-free level playing field can help protect the honest businessman as well as the domestic economy and bureaucrats. Good leaders and decision-makers need such insulation.

Factors that have been identified as corresponding with high levels of corruption include: low public-servant salaries, high tax regimes, heavy-handed, non-transparent regulations over the economy and the environment, low budget transparency, and close co-operation between politicians, the military and big business.

Corruption flourishes where governments are involved in Think Big-type projects, penalising small enterprises that don't have the political and financial muscle to peddle influence. It's easier for officials to skim money off aircraft contracts than school textbooks. Privately owned companies are less likely to be corrupt, but there is a 'special window' of opportunity for theft in the transition towards privatisation. It's about influence peddling, extortion, fraud, grease or speed money paid to officials to speed up the decision-making process, and plain embezzlement.

What then is to be done? The OECD is correct in seeking laws to outlaw bribery to protect honest countries whose honest business people must become dishonest to compete. Lower inflation, reformed tax regimes, better pay for public servants, better examples by political leaders, the advancement of democratic institutions, further deregulation and economic liberalisation, cleaner and more transparent government purchasing procedures, including military procurement and increased budget transparency, are necessary.

All the great institutions need to address this and to support brave leaders, who must see that they can make changes without committing political suicide and risking assassination. It begs the question, how can an honest person be elected in the first place?

Non-governmental Organisations (NGOs)

The birth of great international institutions, laws and treaties will ensure the survival of our species, not just the survival of the fittest. Now we have unleashed the secrets of the atom and have the capacity to destroy our entire existence we need to match that awesome and deadly power with democratic systems to protect one another's interests.

But internationalism is not, and should not be, just the domain of governments and their institutions. The demand for the research and support services of non-governmental organisations (NGOs) has exploded. This should be welcomed by professional policymakers as part of the democratisation of policymaking and its delivery. Frequently they are more effective than governments and can do things governments can't.

From the Red Cross and Oxfam to sports clubs, the Olympic movement, religious organisations, trade unions and business councils there are tens of thousands of invisible networks circling and tying the globe together. That's good. It's not a danger: it's the privatisation of influence from the powerful to the many. God bless the Internet. Governments can no longer control ideas or the people.

Anne-Marie Slaughter from Harvard Law School sees it as 'a shift away from the state – up, down and sideways – to supra-state, sub-state, and, above all, non-state actors. These new players have multiple allegiances and global reach.

The result is not world government, but global governance. If government denotes the formal exercise of power by established institutions, governance denotes co-operative problem-solving by a changing and often uncertain cast. The result is a world order in which global governance networks link Microsoft, the Roman Catholic Church, and Amnesty International to the European Union, the United Nations, and Catalonia.

The state is not disappearing, it is disaggregating into its separate, functionally distinct parts. These parts – courts, regulatory agencies, executives, and even legislatures – are networking with their counterparts abroad, creating a dense web of relations that constitutes a new, transgovernmental order ...

The densest area of transgovernmental activity is among national regulators. Bureaucrats charged with the administration of anti-trust policy, securities regulation, environmental policy, criminal law enforcement, banking and insurance supervision – in short, all the agents of the modern regulatory state – regularly collaborate with their foreign counterparts.[1]

The Treaty-making Process

Citizens of individual countries will not, and should not, accept any form of international regulation or institution over which they have little control. Keeping control of bureaucrats at a domestic level is tough enough: at an international level it will be tougher.

Governments such as New Zealand's will have to make treaty-making more transparent. The nation state should only transfer power when it's in its interests and only with the approval of its Parliaments, people and courts.

In March 1997 I presented a paper to both the Labour caucus and the Foreign Affairs, Defence and Trade Select Committee, seeking to reform the treaty-making process. Our Parliament has no role in scrutinising international treaties before the government signs them, and will only debate them at all if they necessitate a change in our domestic laws. The MAI does not necessitate a law change and therefore there will be no debate. That's wrong and counter-productive.

Parliament should have a constitutional role in the treaty-making process, including scrutiny and ratification of all important international agreements. To be fair, however, the government has recently adopted many of my proposals in this area.

In the end there is no single structure, institution, theory, flow chart or magic bullet. Domestic civil society was painfully built up over centuries by thousands of concerned individuals and their interaction. Trust in law and society's institutions was eventually earned. International civil society will be built on integrity, and respect will be earned on the basis of results. But it's a long, imperfect process.

As the founding father of the EU, Jean Monnet, said:

The only things that can be left to future generations are strong institutions. Disraeli claimed that nations and civil society must be governed by rules and institutions or anarchy and violence.

CHAPTER SIX

Luddites and Leadership:
New Zealand's Response

Yesterday is not ours to recover, but tomorrow is ours to win or lose.
— Lyndon B. Johnson

WHAT SHOULD BE New Zealand's response to the opportunities of this brave new world? Should we pursue democratic internationalism, which advances the rights and role of the nation state while seeking to enable, enfranchise and liberalise, or will we go down the road of ultra-nationalism?

One of the reasons I wrote this book, and an earlier book on New Zealand's *Children of the Poor*, was the fear I had that the agenda for ensuring a growing economy would be captured by the tired old left: those who seek to smuggle back discredited theories and economic models of controls, subsidies, and protectionism – the promise of a better past when coal was king.

At a time of rising civil unrest during the advent of the industrial age, Benjamin Disraeli, later to become one of Britain's greatest prime ministers, wrote a novel called *Sybil*. It was a clever book full of wit, charm, romance and political intrigue, which questioned the values of Victorian Britain. Clichés only become clichés because they are in the main true and Disraeli's phrase 'two nations' has passed into the English language. He warned Britain of the obscene inequalities of the day – from the desperate poverty of industrial workers to the absurd and flamboyant excesses of the very rich.

A passage from his novel reads:

'Well, society may be in its infancy,' said Egremont, slightly smiling, 'but say what you like, the Queen reigns over the greatest nation that ever existed.'

'Which nation?' asked the younger stranger, 'for she reigns over two.'

The stranger paused; Egremont was silent, but looked enquiringly.

'Yes,' resumed the younger stranger after a moment's interval. 'Two nations; between them there is no intercourse and no sympathy; who are as ignorant of each other's habits, thoughts and feelings as if they were dwellers in different zones, or inhabitants of different planets who are formed by a different breeding, are fed by a different food, are ordered by different manners, and are not governed by the same laws.'

'You speak of …' said Egremont, hesitatingly.

'*The rich and the poor.*'

Our modern open economy, critics correctly claim, works for 80 per cent of the people but not for the 20 per cent at the bottom. But the economic nationalist solution will be to abolish the success of the 80 per cent, as though that will help those who have borne the brunt of the restructuring and inter-nationalisation of the New Zealand economy.

It is true that we have failed to make our economy work for enough New Zealanders. But it is equally true that the open economic model has delivered more jobs, opportunities and security to more people than any system yet devised. Nations that embrace trade win; those that don't, lose. Countries that have embraced free trade have doubled the real incomes of their workers in a remarkably short time. That is the undeniable lesson of economic history.

What I am saying will jar with many good social liberals. It's designed to. What is it about trade liberalisation that attracts such public abuse? There is a mutant strain of leftist thought that still believes that private enterprise, trade and business are wicked. Some, like the old Social Crediters, still argue that it is all a global conspiracy. But look what happened to the policies of these people when they were applied after the Wall Street crash of the 1920s. The United States threw up the barriers, exacerbating the world depression that brought misery to millions. A growing, free, world economy is a matter of political, economic and military security.

This confusing new world creates strange bedfellows as, for example, the far right in the US and Ralph Nader form bizarre coalitions to fight the changes that threaten their disappearing world. They are the champions of the dying industrial age.

It is curious that in New Zealand those who oppose economic internation-alism flatter themselves by saying that they are left-wing, whereas in other countries those who oppose economic liberalisation are normally from the right: Le Pen in France, Pat Buchanan in the United States, Pauline Hanson in Australia. The left in New Zealand have borrowed a lot of the literature and arguments used by the extreme right-wing militia types in the US, who believe there is a sinister group of people plotting away trying to make a world government and deny people their individual and national rights.

But the United Nations is not a sinister plot, and nor is the World Trade Organisation. Conspiracy theories are not new; they go back to the protocols of Zion, and the rumblings and emergence of fascism. (Fluoridation was not a commie Catholic plot either.)

I was once abused by a committed and sincere low-paid worker for a worthy group who run Trade Aid, which imports products from developing countries to sell in its shops. She said, 'Before you were government and opened the market we had all the imports from developing countries. Now every Tom, Dick and Harry imports and sells them.' So what's so socialist about making T-shirts dearer for solo parents?

One left-wing MP complained that Nike was moving out of South Korea and Indonesia into China, after all the complaints about labour rights in South Korea (never North Korea). I said that was great, and that I hoped I lived long enough to see labour costs rise so much that China lost business and jobs to Somalia or Ethiopia. That's the whole point of it.

Of course this knee-jerk resistance to change is not a new phenomenon. Earlier we examined how civilisation has passed from hunter-gatherers to an agricultural society, and then to an industrial society. Each turn of this historic wheel saw massive dislocation, hatred and disillusionment with leaders, and was accompanied by violence by those marginalised.

The newest wave of change we now face is just as daunting, and the natural response of many is to want to resist it, especially if they are members of the status quo that enjoys present privileges.

As the social dislocation of this phase of history weakens the power of politicians, governments and conventional capitalists will fight to prevent change and protect their position, just as the monarchs, lords and popes did during previous historical cycles of change.

The pain and problems brought about by change are real for those at the bottom of the heap too. At the time of the 'gunpowder revolution', around the 16th century, incomes dropped by 50 per cent and didn't rise until the industrial revolution. Fertile ground for anger. In 1800 some 80 per cent of Europeans worked on the land: it's now 3 per cent, but much more food is produced. That's a pretty radical change of lifestyle.

The industrial revolution was opposed in turn by those who feared the introduction of 'new technology' such as mechanical looms and water-driven power. These innovations de-skilled many jobs, meaning an idiot and a genius on an assembly line could both produce the same product and earn the same wages. This is when the term luddite came into existence. Last century they gave the British Parliament an ultimatum:

We will never lay down arms [till] The House of Commons passes an Act to put down all Machinery hurtful to Commonality, and repeal that to hang Frame Breakers. ... We petition no more – that won't do – fighting must.

> Signed by the General of the Army of Redressers
> Ned Ludd Clerk
> Redressers for ever, Amen.

Now, as then, the pain is real. Economies and peoples have been devastated and nations destabilised. The people hurt and cry out for comfort. What to do? We are facing a new challenge, never before faced nor fully understood.

There is only one way forward now for nations that want to survive and thrive in the next century. Democracy is the first cousin of adaptability and flexibility, and provides the practical political ability to change and evolve peacefully.

'The duty of leaders is to prepare the people, not to save the past. Coal is no longer king, neither is oil, information is now king,' as Mancur Olson says in *The Rise and Decline of Nations*. 'Peoples who master this complex new world will enjoy its benefits.'

Governments led by luddites, with whom New Zealand is overly blessed, will try to stop the process by clamping in place controls at a domestic level. They will fail. Their trade negotiators in Paris, Brussels or Tokyo will busily draw up rules based on an earlier age and an earlier agenda. Controls won't work, it is technologically impossible. But they can stall progress, thus making the inevitable more costly and painful.

More enlightened leaders will try to grapple with an analysis of the problem and conclude than an internationalist and intergovernmental and interagency response is best.

I believe the advantages of free and fair international trade are overwhelmingly evident, but the debate must still be held, in New Zealand as elsewhere, because we can only go as far as the public allow. The obvious always takes longer, as do short-cuts that don't show the people democratic respect.

Our largest and most conservative newspaper, The *New Zealand Herald*, contributed to the debate a cartoon showing fat, besuited officials with fountain pens on their shoulders like rifles marching through checkpoints.

How shallow. Forget that the great white tribes of Europe and their civil wars have twice this century led us into global war. That an integrated, expanded European Union is now a shining beacon for peace and hope on that tortured continent.

That negative view is sincerely held by many who blame globalisation for the cost of change.

I saw my job as Trade Minister for New Zealand as a chance to do my patriotic duty. I was working for jobs in New Zealand and I saw that pulling down New Zealand's Berlin Wall of import controls would also help transfer wealth to poorer countries in the Pacific. Now that position is more and more portrayed as a betrayal of New Zealand. From hero to traitor in a decade! I was in part driven to write this book because of that perception.

Davidson and Rees-Mogg in *The Sovereign Individual* predicted just such a reaction:

> Even countries that have been at the forefront of reform and stand to benefit disproportionately from 'market-friendly globalism', like New Zealand, will be tormented by reactionary losers. They will seek to thwart the movement of capital and people across borders. And they will not stop there … They will seek to halt the diffusion of computers, robotics, telecommunications, encryption, and other Information Age technologies that are facilitating the displacement of workers in almost every sector of the global economy. … demagogues will rail against the globalisation of markets, immigration, and freedom of investment.

The first phase of New Zealand's liberalisation was appropriate but it came at great pain and the costs fell unfairly. We all know that. Yet although you can save old jobs by protection for a short time, ultimately that starves investment in new jobs. You end up with neither new jobs nor old jobs. That was the lesson of the 1970s.

Most of the changes since the 1980s have been good. We are positioning ourselves well. Inefficiencies in our transport and port system were identified as a major barrier, a tax on producers, exporters and importers. That's why we reorganised the waterfront. Our strategy, managed by Transport Minister Bill Jeffries, resulted in port ownership transferred to local authorities with the abolition of harbour boards.

Port owners, operators, users and other identified beneficiaries of reform were levied to pay for the cost of restructuring, including redundancies.

By 1990 New Zealand's waterfront was 60 per cent cheaper to run than Australia's. Cargo handling costs had been reduced by 66 per cent. Labour gangs were 20-40 per cent smaller. Record cargo loading rates were being set every few weeks. Annual cost savings had reached $58 million. Average port stays for vessels had been reduced by more than 50 per cent.

By 1992 New Zealand watersiders were able to unload 35 containers an hour compared with eight an hour in Australia. Port charges in Tauranga in 1992 averaged A\$4387 per vessel compared with A\$21,813 in Australia. Charges for taking paper cargo across a wharf cost A\$4 per tonne in New Zealand compared with A\$24 in Australia. No one was sacked, many workers over 50 took early retirement. There was no Employment Contracts Act.

The same strategy was implemented for telecommunications. Inefficiencies in that sector were stifling innovation, frustrating investors and were a toll gate – a judder bar – on the road to progress.

Fifteen years ago, who would have predicted that the New Zealand Dairy Board would beat Nestlé in South East Asia? Anyone who doubts that New Zealand has much to gain from being part of the global economy should glance through the board's latest annual report.

Worldwide sales of the board's consumer products reached 260,000 tonnes in 1996-97, generating \$1.4 billion or 23 per cent of the board's total revenues. Specialised protein ingredients from New Zealand are key components in a growing range of sport nutrition products in Japan. The board's United States subsidiary has developed an exciting new high-calcium milk protein product suitable for multiple applications, such as in coffee creamers.

Having established brand leadership in Russia with Anchor butter, the board has moved into the branded cheese market. New technology developed in New Zealand has given the board access to the huge fresh cheese market in Mexico. A New Zealand milk powder developed to meet the special nutritional needs of pregnant mothers is selling in five South East Asian markets. And in Sri Lanka, where Anchor already has market dominance, the board has launched a new yoghurt range. The board has recently commissioned new plants in El Salvador and Mexico, is building a new plant in Malaysia and has set up a new marketing company in Portugal.

New Zealand can become an example to the world. Rees-Mogg and Davidson see

> ... much more attractive prospects for doing business in areas where indebtedness is low and governments have already been restructured, such as New Zealand, Argentina, Chile, Peru, Singapore, and other parts of Asia and Latin America. These areas will also be superior platforms for doing business to unreformed, high-cost economies in North America and Western Europe.

The call for a reversal is the target of some in the Alliance, as it was for National in the 1990 election. Why do the so-called radicals stick to policies that were radical 50 years ago? They are the new conservatives. Welsh socialist and visionary Aneurin Bevan warned in *In Place of Fear* of the need to

> … guard against the old words for the words persist when the reality that lay behind them has changed. It is inherent in our intellectual activity that we seek to imprison reality in our description of it. Soon, long before we realise it, it is we who become the prisoners of the prescription. From that point on, our ideas degenerate into a kind of folklore which we pass to each other, fondly thinking we are still talking of the reality around us.

No one said it would be easy. Robert H. Waterman studies businesses that have succeeded and those that failed. In his book *The Renewal Factor* he explains:

> Habit breaking, the requisite for change and renewal needs more than a simple decision to do it. It takes motivation, desire and will. Crisis can provide that. But the leaders of renewing organisations seem to get their determination from their singular ability to anticipate crisis. That stems from their continuing willingness to look into 'a different mirror'.
>
> Those renewing companies get their passport to reality stamped regularly. Their leaders listen. They are open, curious, and inquisitive. They get ideas from customers, suppliers, front line employers, competitors, politicians – almost anyone outside the hierarchy. An executive at a high-tech company said that one different mirror for him was serving on the board of a declining company in smokestack America. 'That whole industry seems trapped in a disastrous set of habits,' he remarked. 'It has made me especially sensitive to the habit patterns that will make or break us.'

This is as true for countries as it is for companies.

The anti-foreign investment or anti-immigration flag is a sign of a deeper racist impulse among voters. There's always a group in every country that plays this card. ACT in New Zealand is now in on the game, ever so subtly calling for 'property rights': a thinly disguised challenge to treaty rights.

The nasty ultra-nationalists are the most obvious: they use the race card blatantly, suggesting that all the problems (be it Indonesia, or pre-war Germany) are caused because of the ethnic Chinese, or Jewish merchants. Imagine if all the members of the New Zealand Business Roundtable were Chinese, Spanish or Muslim. The talkbacks would have a field day! New Zealanders are not as clean or green as we would like to think.

At the other extreme our progress has been hindered by those who pro-

91

mote the philosophy of economic rationalism or the law of the market jungle. Imagine driving down Wall Street in New York without traffic lights or pedestrian crossings!

Unfortunately, free-market policies in New Zealand have been taken to an intellectual extreme. The market is not an ideology or a philosophy. It is an instrument, a mechanism like the combustion engine, but someone must drive it. The market is simply a collection of values, rules, precedents and opportunities. It is not all-powerful; it cannot achieve miracles; its prescriptions are not written by Dr God.

Trade and the market alone cannot provide a redistribution mechanism for wealth. Yet there are those in New Zealand who now use the market as an excuse for doing nothing. If something needed to be done the market would do it, they argue, thus there is no need for government.

It reminds me of the story of two professors at Chicago University wandering around the campus and talking about the theory of rational expectations. One of them saw a $100 note on the ground and said, 'Look, there is a hundred dollars!' The other one said, 'Nonsense, under the theory of rational expectations somebody would have picked it up by now.'

I remember putting up a paper saying that for every dollar spent in Tradenz and trade promotion I got $4 back. I sought a budget increase. Treasury replied saying if this was true I didn't need the dollar.

ACT is the closest New Zealand has to an anarchist party. Its zealous supporters believe that if the state disappears entirely so will the country's problems. They miss the point. It's simplistic nonsense, but then most extremist theologies are.

The market is not perfect: its philosophy isn't God-given, God-driven. The more extreme free-market ideologues are like the old communists who, if the policies were not working, claimed it was because people didn't believe in them enough. They had to go faster, get up earlier. Expel and excommunicate the disbelievers.

Let us not lose sight of the fact that public-good policies last century, for example collective provision of sewerage systems and running water, greatly enhanced quality of life and increased life expectancy. Public education liberated people from the rigidities of class confinement and unleashed the talents of the wider populace, which in turn generated new wealth and growth.

The modern welfare state liberated millions of people's skills, ideas and abilities and gave an enormous impetus for growth by freeing up education and providing public works such as health and transport infrastructure. Prime Minister Norman Kirk once said: 'Social security does not imprison people, it sets them free. It does not sap self-reliance. It strengthens confidence by removing fear and security.'

Yet Seddon, Savage and Kirk, the pioneers of New Zealand's welfare state, could never have foreseen a time when one in three would be on a benefit. It was to be a hand-up when things were seasonally tough, not a full-time occupation.

Within 25 years, one-quarter of New Zealanders will be eligible for New Zealand Superannuation alone, yet the first retirement scheme, designed in Germany by Bismarck, envisaged only 2.5 per cent of the population being covered. Some 80 per cent of people in parts of the East Coast of New Zealand are on welfare benefits.

Putting people on benefits is the modern version of putting coins in the plate at church on Sunday. It's not good enough any more. Throughout the world politicians everywhere, including President Clinton, are promising to redesign the welfare state. Because the welfare state is in disrepair and doesn't work.

The role of the state is pivotal in preparing its people to face the future. The New Zealand government has to educate, prepare, educate and prepare. Knock down the barriers that will otherwise cost us the future, whether they are regulations, tariffs or attitudes. Learn from those who have thought it through and remember the lessons hard learnt by our grandparents.

Economic failure, weakness in international law and institutions gave us the Great Depression and world war, which in turn gave us the twin tyrannies of our age, fascism and Marxism. The killing fields of Cambodia and the tyrant Pol Pot were born out of military and economic failure, allowing the ultimate ultra-nationalist to drive his peaceful country into a nightmare it still has not recovered from. That this monster died peacefully (we are told) so recently says a lot about us all.

CHAPTER SEVEN

Future-proofing New Zealand

Free-marketism and trickle-downism twisted into rigid theological dogma are
inadequate responses to the Third Wave. A party facing the future should be
warning of problems to come and suggesting preventative change.
— Alvin Toffler, *Creating a New Civilization*

POLITICS AND POLITICAL parties in New Zealand are still stuck in the industrial age. Politics in the future will not be divided by the old boundaries of left and right – they have as much relevance today as the old battles between the Protestants and the Catholics in Europe, or the 100 Years War. These days it is about those who understand that the industrial age is dead, and those who do not. The difference will be in the response to that profound reality.

The invention and development of refrigeration revolutionised New Zealand. It changed everything. The information age will do the same. Information technology has made it possible for us to connect and work with more people in more locations around the world. To quote the Singaporean Minister of Education, 'Our world has shrunk; and so must our minds expand to learn to take in all that is now within our reach.'

Education is the key. There is little place in the modern economy for unskilled or semi-skilled workers. If all you have to sell is a strong pair of hands, you will not have much of a future.

An OECD report released in April 1998 warned that half of New Zealand's workforce is not literate enough to work in a modern economy. Around the same time the World Competitiveness Report showed that New Zealand had slipped from 9th to 13th place overall since 1995 and key indicators such as domestic economic performance and infrastructure adequacy had fallen even further.

That same month the result of the Third International Maths and Science Study, which looked at the maths and science performance of nine-year-olds from 40 countries, placed New Zealand students on a similar level to those from Thailand, Cyprus and Greece. Their performance fell below that of students from Australia, the US and Japan. Just over a third of the students tested made it over the halfway mark. Some 20 per cent of New Zealand children have reading levels below their age expectations.

New Zealand lags behind its competitors, who don't sleep. A child in Singapore or Taiwan has three times more chance of getting a university degree than a Kiwi kid.

We need to ensure that our children are receiving an education that not only equips them with information and technology skills, but that also 'future-proofs' them with the skills to anticipate and cope with change.

The Singapore government has launched a public programme to rewire its nation. Every school, business and home is part of this ambitious plan.

Too small to rely on its own resources, Singapore now knows that its once competitive advantage of location is becoming less relevant. They have created a multibillion-dollar initiative called 'The IT2000 Vision of an Intelligent Island'.

In so doing, Singapore has deliberately prepared itself to meet the challenges of the information age. A positive environment now exists for the private and public sectors to collaborate in exploiting IT for national competitive advantage. The World Competitiveness Report has, in recent years, placed Singapore among the top nations in the world in terms of strategic exploitation of IT by companies, computer literacy of workers and telecommunications infrastructure.

IT2000 will see Singapore, some 15 years from now, among the first countries in the world with an advanced nationwide information infrastructure. It will interconnect computers in virtually every home, office, school and factory. The computer will evolve into an information appliance, combining the functions of the telephone, computer, TV and more. It will provide a wide range of communication means and access to services.

Singapore's programme was conceived after a rigorous study covering the country's 11 major economic sectors: construction and real estate; education and training; financial services; government; health care; the IT industry; manufacturing; media, publishing and information services; retail, wholesale and distributional tourism and leisure services; and transport.

The study tapped the practical and visionary expertise of more than 200 senior executives from both the public and private sectors to see how IT could be pervasively applied to improve business performance and quality of life.

The Singaporean Minister of Education, Radm Teo Chee Hean, launched Singapore's masterplan in April 1997, explaining:

As a young boy in primary school it seemed to me that my school was huge. The hall was a big cavernous space and the school field was a large sea of green, or brown if it had not rained for a while, stretching out to the fence which was the boundary of our world. We lived in this world, guided by our principal and teachers. Many years later, having grown up and seen the world outside, I returned to the school for a gathering of old boys. It seemed like not such a big place after all – in fact, quite a small, cosy place …

The world has changed. Technology has changed it. We are now able to reach out from our schoolrooms to any place in the world. The only fences are in our minds …

To thrive in this future world of the 21st century, Singaporeans must learn to think beyond the bounds of their physical surroundings – beyond home and school, to the community, our country, our region and the wider world. Singaporeans must also learn to think beyond the obvious, to think creatively, to search for new technologies and be able to exploit these new technologies to venture beyond their current.

It is a brave new plan that has every chance of success. And Singapore is not alone. Germany, Italy, France and Finland all have major plans to ensure their environments become smart through smart education and new forms of schooling. Malaysia's 'supercorridor', designed to attract investment and high-tech companies, is a brave, visionary attempt to become the region's leader.

Britain's Prime Minister Tony Blair's ambitious plan means that by the year 2002 all schools will be connected to the information superhighway, free of charges. Half a million teachers will be retrained, and every child will leave school IT literate.

Blair is targeting poorer schools first. The result is that truancy has dropped. Is that startling? Perhaps only to those who are so out of touch with human nature that they fail to appreciate that boredom and low self-esteem lie at the root of much of what we would characterise as the anti-social behaviour of youth, of which truancy is but one example. Consider the words of David Wimpress, the managing director of ICL Education:

Trouble-making boys love to use computers, which means that at times when they would be a problem, such as in the playground, they are tapping away. Truancy in the largest school has fallen by 10 per cent. And it can boost self-esteem of low-achievers. If their handwriting is bad, or they can't spell, this doesn't matter because they can use a piece of software to present their work better, and to submit a piece as good as their classmates.

The UK National Learning Grid, which is managing these changes, identified its biggest problem as transcending the inertia of government departments. What New Zealand needs to counter a similar kind of inertia is leaders of vision.

The great public works of the past in New Zealand were the railways of Vogel, and the roads of Bob Semple. Where is the political visionary who will lay down the new information highway for NZew Zealand? Or will student fees be a toll gate that prices the young off the road? The lack of planning for future infrastructural needs, social, intellectual and physical, is proving very costly.

Auckland's power crisis in early 1998 showed up the political short-sightedness of postponing or sidelining basic public works, the unseen support structures of sewerage, transport, electricity and school buildings that we take for granted until they collapse.

At rush hour it takes 45 minutes to cross the Auckland Harbour Bridge. Queues stretch up to six kilometres. Without public transport the queues would be 21 kilometres long, yet the National government has cut millions from public transport.

What is the cost to Auckland – and to New Zealand – of Auckland's congested and inefficient traffic system? What's the cost to people and business if 300,000 motor vehicles are delayed each day for 15 minutes? Ernst & Young, a respected international group of consultants, put the cost of Auckland's traffic congestion at $755 million a year.

Add to that the total of unrecovered costs, i.e. those not picked up by insurance companies or ACC, which for the whole of New Zealand is estimated to be $525 million. Then add Auckland's share of pollution and CO_2 emission costs, which nationally is estimated at $355 million. Why not add a bit for motor accidents, because US authorities say 66 per cent of all traffic accidents arise from road rage. Then it is quite easy to suggest that the real cost to Auckland, and New Zealand, of Auckland's traffic problem is $1 billion a year.

Wellington's roading delays cost $100 million a year. Local body politicians love to build town halls and entertainment centres because that's where the votes are – until there's a disaster like the Auckland power crisis. Politicians generally, fearing electorate revolt, promise 'no new taxes', thus conspiring to cheat and pass on this real infrastructural debt to future generations. The interest on this debt is the hidden cost of inefficiency. Central government has cut the real level of public involvement by 20 per cent since National took office in 1990.

This has seriously affected schools and universities. Overcrowded classrooms and maintenance postponed make for a cleaner balance sheet but creates an educational skills deficit that credit ratings agencies such as Moody's can't see. The governor of the Reserve Bank was moved to comment in June 1998 that this skills deficit was one of the reasons the New Zealand economy was not growing as fast as predicted.

In 1998 Canterbury was reeling under a drought while rivers rushed millions of tons of water to the sea. Observers noting the high rainfall on the West Coast often suggest the water be pumped over the Southern Alps to Canterbury and Central Otago. A Snowy River scheme for New Zealand. A Labour member of the Upper House in the 1940s once suggested we use these 'new-fangled nuclear bombs' to flatten the alps and make New Zealand a third bigger. Oh dear. Still, it was Labor that promoted the White Australia policy, but then it was Labor in office that reversed it. We learn.

There's no need to pump water over the alps: Canterbury has rivers – the Ashley, the Rakaia, the Waimakariri. Look at the Israelis. Their nation is the same size as the province of Canterbury, and they changed their nation by prudent use of water. By bringing together environmentalists, Maori and farmers, we could find a way to solve our problem. That's where local and national government come in, called upon to act for the public good. Every great journey begins with a single step and that's the hardest step to take. Irrigation investment is the longest-term investment you can ever make. It can take 20 years to get a return from a tree. Some New Zealand farmers are still getting a return from irrigation runs made 100 years ago. The irrigation schemes of ancient civilisations are still giving a return to growers in Sri Lanka and China.

These stirring words were read out by disgraced Australian Mineral Minister Rex Connor when he resigned his portfolio after the loans affair, where he had tried, without Cabinet or Treasury approval, to raise capital from Iraq to develop Australia:

> Give me men to match my mountains,
> Give me men to match my plains,
> Men with freedom in their vision,
> And creation in their brains.

I'm not advocating a Bill Birch Think Big scale of development, but I am saying that we need a bold, environmentally acceptable and sustainable agricultural infrastructure. The funding for such a scheme is a matter for the beneficiaries, not the taxpayer, but the initiative must be the government's.

To impress the money markets with our fiscal deficit target, we have been blowing out our real deficits in our physical, intellectual and social infrastructure. The potential cost of this in the future is incalculable.

On the other hand, much energy has gone into restructuring and corporatising government services. This has by and large been a good thing. But the public service is not an end in itself: it's there to provide a service to its owners, the people. Inefficiencies represent money and services denied its owners. Bringing in outside managers and putting staff on contracts is generally a good idea. But the explosion of new, highly qualified, private-sector managers created distortions and an unreal atmosphere that snowballed costs at the top and the expense to those at the bottom.

The old public service deal was that wages were traded for security. With corporatisation public service managers become yuppies, got new names for their departments, together with flash new logos and advertising campaigns. Soon they were comparing themselves with the private corporate world, seeking salary packages and often bonuses based on how many workers and services they could cut. Greed was good: it was the 1980s.

But people need the reassurance of symbols and structures they feel comfortable with. We knew and liked State Advances, but it became the Housing Corporation and then Housing New Zealand. Social Welfare became Income Support. Once we had hospitals, then they were turned into Crown health enterprises. Why?

The public service ethic is eroding. One departmental paper suggested that because the head of Income Support handled a budget as big as the largest public company, he should get the same pay as his so-called private-sector counterpart. A person from Lotto suggested to me they should be in the Fortune 500 and be rewarded accordingly because per head of staff they had a huge turnover and profit. 'What?' I replied. 'You run a *monopoly* raffle! On that reasoning, why shouldn't the head of Inland Revenue get the highest pay? Surely they have the highest turnover per person in the country!'

As private-sector wage differences grow, so do disparities in the public sector. Judges claim that since there are now many million-dollar lawyers, why not them? The Higher Salaries Commission, which sets the wages of MPs, judges and certain other public servants, surveys the private sector as a comparison, so the disparities flow on and feed off each other. This tests public confidence, trust and social cohesion.

Now you can't find out what ministers' advisers and press secretaries get paid because of 'commercial confidentiality', yet at the same time we have passed laws giving shareholders in public companies the right to know what they are paying their CEOs. Ministers frequently won't answer questions in Parliament on the basis of commercial confidentiality, now that much work is contracted out. So the democratic deficit builds, the distrust grows. Their owners and shareholders are you, the people, and you have been forgotten.

Public-sector reform got out of hand. It should have got a mark of 9, but it got a 7 because of the attitudes and actions of those at the top.

Labour's greatest failure in its reform from 1984 to 1990 was the reality that people didn't feel that the burdens were fairly shared. And that was partly true. It's more true now. Our tax system gives comfort to the richest. How is it that companies can indulge in orgies of takeovers, subsidised by ordinary taxpayers?

And today the more money you have the more you can play games with family trusts and creative investment. The very wealthy never paid the super-annuation surcharge. Most Cabinet ministers have family trusts so they and their parents will not have to sell off their assets in order to claim health and geriatric care.

The fringe benefit tax was a good step in taxing perks such as cars, executive suites at the football, medical insurance and overseas trips. It's fine if companies want to fund these extravagances, but why should the taxpayer? It's corporate welfare and it's a rip-off. But there's no TV campaign urging 'good citizens' to ring up and dob in tax fraud as there is for benefit fraud.

Workers under siege feel sickened when they see the Business Roundtable attack redundancy payouts to workers and decisions of the Employment Court, and want to pass retrospective legislation to abolish agreements entered into by free negotiation. Confiscating wealth is called nationalisation; abolishing workers' conditions is called progress and freedom.

Let the employers have their multimillion-dollar payouts and salaries, but why should we fund them out of taxes? They should not be written off as a business cost. It's these contradictions that give validity to calls of hypocrisy. Belt-tightening is best led by example. The explosion of Maori capitalism based on Treaty of Waitangi settlements will also see shareholders begin to bring their leaders to account.

It's time to have another go at corporate and bureaucratic bludgers.

If the family is the basic social and economic unit (as promoted by politicians and recognised by every great religion and culture throughout history) why are the family and children not adequately recognised in our tax code?

Yvonne and I have no children, this is our greatest tragedy. But given that there are only two of us, we should pay more tax than a couple on a similar income with five children – they have seven mouths to feed. In time these children will be paying tax of their own. People without children should pay more tax than family people.

Yes, family people get more back for their tax dollars from the health and education system, because of their children. But who's going to look after us in our old age? The ageing of the population is a worldwide phenomenon in sophisticated economies. Alexander the Great was an old man of 30 when he conquered the known world (and what a Eurocentric statement that is!). We spend more health dollars in the last two years of our lives than in all the other years put together.

We need a funded savings scheme for retirement. Alas, the Winston Peters scheme was not the Norman Kirk scheme. Mind you, at the time Mr Peters could not sell a cold beer on a troopship in the tropics. He was judged. In politics it's often the author, not the book, that's judged.

A side benefit of a compulsory savings and superannuation scheme would be that if a government wanted to slow down the economy at certain times of the economic cycle it could decide to increase the rate of some people's investment in retirement. High-income people, who could afford it, could be encouraged to increase their savings rate so as to reach the target of savings necessary to fund their retirement earlier.

People would keep these savings, which would result in less pressure on interest rates. The Reserve Bank governor would have to take that into consideration in maintaining whatever contract on inflation he's agreed to with the Treasurer.

New Zealand's interest rates are high partly because of our low savings. This is why we need the savings of more prudent people overseas for investment. The problem in Japan is exactly the opposite: tax cuts are often saved rather than spent and therefore do little to boost domestic consumer demand.

If taking money out of circulation to slow inflation growth is the imperative, why don't we simply increase tax? Because government programmes would simply expand and the money would end up back in the economy in a most inefficient way. It takes the foot off the throats of government departments and expenditure discipline. It lowers the confidence of the market because they have seen it all before.

Every 10 years I suggest a compulsory savings and superannuation scheme at Labour caucus, and lose. Why the New Zealand trade union movement is so opposed mystifies me. Who owns the US? Says Peter Drucker in his book *The Pension Fund Revolution*, workers through their pension funds own more of American business than 'Allende in Chile ever brought under state ownership, or Castro nationalised, or was ever owned by the state of Hungary and Poland at the height of Stalinism'.

US pension funds hold one-tenth of the equity capital in US publicly owned companies, 40 per cent of the common stock of the nation's large and medium businesses, and 40 per cent of the medium- and long-term debt of its bigger companies. If socialism is defined by the ownership of the means of production, the US is the most socialised economy ever.

Our Reserve Bank Act is good, open and transparent. But let's not pretend that the contract between the government and the governor is not an intervention and a basic contradiction of free-market principles. The bank's governor makes his interest rate calls based on all the factors that exist in an economy at any one time. When I was briefly prime minister I put together a growth agreement with the unions (against the advice of the experts). The governor of the Reserve Bank was basing his inflation estimates on a 5 per cent wage increase. By agreement with the union this came down to 2 per cent, with all other increases to be based on productivity improvements. This was no pipe dream: major unions such as the Waterfront and Engineers settled for such figures. Hey presto, the assumptions changed, interest rates could be lowered, inflation targets preserved. Alas, not in time to save my government of eight weeks. I can assure readers that the concept of receiving 'a suicide pass' is alive and well in professional politics, just as in professional rugby. The point the two professions have in common is clear: no matter what you see looming in front of you, you are still expected to catch the ball.

(Ken Douglas and Rex Jones are almost alone among New Zealand union leaders who can see beyond the battle cry of the last class war. Ken's an old Marxist, but his exposure to the ICFTU and a Marxist sweep of history has meant that like many other Kiwis, his reputation is higher abroad than at home.)

Why can't we change other assumptions without changing inflation targets? Why should farmers in the South Island or retailers in Gisborne or small manufacturers in Wellington pay higher interest rates because of a property boom in some parts of Auckland due to immigration? Immigration can be planned, properties can be subdivided to lower prices, changing again interest rate assumptions.

Sado-monetarism uses interest rates as a tool to control money supply and is a blunt weapon. Sure, it drives down the supply of money, affecting homeowners first, but they will recover. Where it damages long-range economic growth is in the areas of business investment in plant and employment, research and development, marketing. New products and new market penetration are postponed. Boards become very conservative, looking at the bottom line and unforgiving shareholders.

Labour lost all moral authority when politicians' wages went up and tax cuts gave the richest the most. That struck at the social cohesion of the country. Those with the most got the most. Social cohesion is central to a successful society, as is the authority of leaders who have to make hard decisions. We want a leaner, not a meaner government. But it was not Labour who cut benefits and raised state house rents to market levels for people who didn't get market wages. Nor did we introduce the Employment Contracts Act, which took from the new, open economy the balancing power of a free, democratic and progressive trade union movement with its feet on the ground and its backside at the board table.

For working people their wages and conditions represent their social capital saved and fought for over generations. To strip them of their assets through the Employment Contracts Act is as vicious as nationalising the bosses' property without compensation. A virile, progressive, democratic modern trade union movement is a vital component of an open economy. Without it, labour is consistently devalued and workers asked to absorb more than their share of the pain of adjustment. It's like running a justice system without legal aid for the victims of the crime and the accused.

The whole employment scene today is radically changed and the pace of that change will accelerate. The most successful retail chain in New Zealand is The Warehouse. Its success is, in part, because it doesn't have a warehouse. Thousands of products sourced cheaply from around the world arrive on its cart dock. It's called Just in Time inventory. Saves on the cost of carrying stock and is based on an efficient transport and computer-based inventory. Goods go straight from the truck to the shop shelves. Corner dairies couldn't handle the inventory of tens of thousands of products now available. Several thousand new products become available every week.

We are now experiencing 'Just in Time employment', with labour on call:

part-time wages for full-time work. Part-time jobs have burgeoned in all Western countries. While this is welcomed by some, it's a menace for many. Working conditions are eroded. You can't look after a family or organise a future on many service-sector wages.

The sobering and most frightening question in all this is what will happen to those workers and families who are in the bottom quintile? Those who leave school without qualifications? Those who for centuries have sold their sweat and muscle? Many of the jobs traditionally available in general labouring have disappeared, many others have become part time, particularly in the service sector. Tertiary students have monopolised many of these jobs such as bar work and fast foods. They have no long-term interest in making the job full time, or advancing workers' conditions. With rising tertiary costs they need the money, not the struggle.

Unskilled workers in the forests, the freezing works and in New Zealand Rail were hit hardest in the reforms of the 1980s. That's true not only of New Zealand. It is global phenomenon as we move from the industrial society to the information age. Alas, Maori and Pacific Islanders were over-represented among the victims. This is the shameful truth of minorities and indigenous people in most societies, Marxist and capitalist.

Maori are over-represented in all the worst statistics – 30 per cent are unemployed in some regions, crime is through the roof, the prisons are bursting and the health statistics shameful. Maori are three to four times more likely to seek treatment for diabetes, 32 per cent of Maori die due to smoking, and two-thirds of pregnant Maori women smoke.

The hard reality is that many jobs simply no longer exist. The answer is not to re-employ 20,000 people on rail or increase the number of freezing workers or wharfies, which we halved. Productivity has become uncoupled from employment. No party, or person, can change this. Up until now growth meant jobs. Now, it's only partly true. New technologies and the international competitive drive mean downsizing to seize and maintain a competitive cost advantage.

Semi-dumb machines and narrowly or semi-skilled workers have little place in the modern economy – unless you want to lower the price of labour beneath that of technology. That's a futile and short-lived advantage. So training and retraining become crucial tools for the future. There's no future at all if all you have to sell are strong hands and sweat.

Tax write-offs and depreciation allowances exist for equipment such as tractors, computers, printing machines, even hotels. The idea is that to keep ahead businesses have to keep purchasing new equipment, even more important, given the advances in technology. That makes sense.

But no such attractive tax regime exists if a company wishes to invest in training and skills. A business gets an incentive to get a new machine, but not a similar incentive to train someone to work the machine. Thus, staff are laid off, made redundant and the company frequently employs someone from a competitor that has made the investment in training. That creates a downward movement in skills training. Employers cannot capture their investment in labour. People are more mobile than ever.

A system of industry levies for training purposes would go a long way towards redressing this imbalance. Any industry that invests, say, 5 per cent of its turnover in training provision would be exempt from this government levy. With the proceeds from the levy, government would augment this training provision in other industries. The hope would be that industry would lift its play rather than send the money to the bureaucrats to spend. The German apprenticeship scheme, where youngsters work three days for industry and then do two days' state-funded training is also worthy of study.

This is the problem all modern economies face as they wrestle with work-for-the-dole schemes and establish training schemes that mostly fail. Kids go from work scheme to work scheme, expectations raised, then cruelly crushed. Training is not enough.

We are going to have to establish new forms of public works – large-scale conservation and cultural works. This must be long term, firmly audited and tightly managed. (And not run by bureaucrats and politicians.) Hundreds of square miles of second-generation bush can be turned into forests. This is the time to utilise this 'surplus labour' to make our streets safer and our communities more liveable. The dole has to be short term: a financial hand-up until real work is found.

In my previous book, *Children of the Poor,* I wrote of a lawn-mowing, football-playing democracy. That is not as trite as it might sound. Societies with strong networks of clubs and organisations have less crime, stronger families, more productive businesses and happier people. We need to re-invent these traditions and give new life to this traditionally Kiwi way of doing things. The fourth Labour government created more than 20,000 Neighbourhood Watch groups, encouraging people to work with their neighbours to combat crime. It worked. Where these groups got together, crime dropped. Such initiatives also have a wider spin-off for the community. They help to cure loneliness, and strengthen families and communities.

We are wasting too many people. Why not encourage those in retirement, or close to retirement, to help us all out? Many do now: it is predominantly the elderly and late middle-aged who run the raffles, meals on wheels and the clubs. There are many organisations that have at their centre a core group of professionals, many with military or police backgrounds: the Red Cross, fire service, coastguard, St John's, surf lifesavers, Civil Defence.

Backed up by an invaluable network of volunteers, these clubs and organisations are a large part of what holds our society together. Why not encourage some people to retire early, give their job to a young person and then pay them a little to help out in the community to reorganise and give life to our civic organisations? Let's say to young unemployed people, many of whom are at risk, that if you can't find a job we want you to help organise and work for St John's, or a local club or beautification society, for a few days a week.

Much of our working, sexual, social and family lives can be summed up as 'participation without commitment'. There is a vast army that participates in great All Black and America's Cup victories and telethons, but too often as an audience of one or two. People want to be neighbours and want to be involved, but do not know how, or they fear personal engagement. That is why soap operas and talkbacks are so popular. It is participation without commitment.

The challenge for the New Zealand government, as for all other governments of the world, is to make the transition to the new information age different. Because we have learnt we have more information, and know it must be done so that the people share both the costs and the benefits fairly. On this rests the tranquillity, cohesion and progress of the nation.

The genius of modern democracy is that change can be predicted and peacefully catered for. Power changes hands without pain. Successful countries and leaders cushion change to protect, assist and retrain the vulnerable and prepare for the inevitable future. Unsuccessful economies resist change with leaders who promise a rosy past. The present is the status quo, and that was yesterday's compromise.

Why do politicians always top the polls of those professions that lie the most? Because those who promise a better past, as demanded by an anxious electorate, in the end can't deliver. No one can. But focus groups, run by pollsters, love these ideas and sophisticated politicians respond to that demand.

More expenditure, lower taxes! The old cliche that power corrupts and absolute power is even more fun is wrong. Power doesn't corrupt: it's what politicians do to get power that corrupts. It's the absence of power that cripples principles.

Government in New Zealand is not historically seen as the enemy as it is in the US and other countries. Our history is different. We are a small country, the government is close by. Our isolation meant we had to do things for ourselves. It wasn't philosophical or ideological: we did what worked. Our rural nature had shown that co-operation at lambing, shearing or hay-baling time was efficient. We established co-operative freezing works, dairy and fertiliser factories.

The government seemed the best and frequently the only organisation capable of building roads, wharves, dams and railways. New Zealand was settled in an orderly fashion. There was no Oklahoma land rush. The pioneers did not come to New Zealand to create a new world. They wanted to replicate the best of the rural old world. The new wave of immigrants don't come to create a new order, they seek riches of a safer, more peaceful nature.

Government and public service can be a positive agent for change. Democracy gives the people the power and responsibility to elect leaders who can look beyond vested interest groups to the horizon. (It's curious that those who use the phrase 'nanny state' as an expletive are always those rich enough to afford nannies.)

In the end the only real job security workers have is the profitability of the business that employs them. We can't tax business losses. The only real economic security a nation can enjoy is financial surpluses, and the savings, skills and confidence of its people. This is especially true in tough times such as the Asian crisis threatens to spread.

The right wing argue government is bad, then run government affairs badly to prove their point. It's not that government in principle is bad. It's just that governments everywhere are incapable of controlling the changes that are being thrust upon us. We need not lose our faith in a democratic purpose. It's the type of response that must change.

It can be boiled down to what makes a New Zealander. I've heard it said that a New Zealander is someone who works for IBM, drives a Japanese car, dreams of a new German car, wears an Italian suit made in Singapore of Australian wool, checks his Swiss watch, adjusts his shorts which are made in China, picks up his Korean-made cellphone and makes a call on an American-owned telecommunications company to complain to his member of Parliament about overseas ownership. His MP, is, of course, doing a study tour of Europe.

That's the negative, protected, frightened description of a Kiwi. My New Zealander is the producer/performer who is so good that the Australian government wanted to stop our TV shows from being allowed to compete with theirs. A dairy farmer or cheese producer whose product is so superior that the US is frightened to do a free trade deal. A butter producer whose innovation in spreadable butter strikes fear into the heart of Brussels bureaucrats. One of 20,000 New Zealanders who work in Asia, investing more in Asia than Asia does in New Zealand.

My New Zealander is one of the 40 per cent of New Zealand school children who are learning another language. A brewer who has opened plants in Australia and China and now produces more beer offshore than onshore and is bold enough to form a global brewing power and merge with a Japanese producer. Someone who feels as confident in Samoa or Kuala Lumpur as they do in Liverpool or Paris. Someone who is proud of the role their nation has played in helping draft the Antarctic Agreement, the Law of the Sea, and the ban on driftnet fishing.

A person who understands that the various cultures, languages and ethnic groups that his children now rub shoulders with in schools will give us a unique ability to do business, talk peace and communicate with other nationalities in the future. Someone who has a sense of pride that his country has been among the first to face the ghosts of its colonial past by addressing the rights of indigenous people through the Treaty of Waitangi. My kind of New Zealander invented the jetboat, and split the atom, and gives more per head of population by free will to telethons and overseas aid groups than any other nation.

A New Zealander is a citizen of a country that in a very short time has come to be among the front line of nations in terms of its living standards based on products such as the cow, the sheep, the kiwifruit, radiata pine and the rugby ball; none of which was native to his land but imported, improved and exported.

When a New Zealander looks outward, he's unbeatable; he can win the America's Cup, then build an export industry based on boat-building worth tens of millions of dollars, reorganise the post office at the same time, then sell that technical experience overseas. When he looks inwards, assumes the

108

foetal position, and pulls the economic and cultural blankets over his head, he's unbearable.

To break this historic mould and cycle of reaction, despair and distress will require serious thought, debate and planning, led by people of vision, wisdom, and leadership. That's an oxymoron. We are in deep trouble.

CHAPTER EIGHT

Best Mates: Australia and the South Pacific

NO NATION IS more important to New Zealand than Australia, for very good reason. No two nations have more in common.

An Australian minister once called in a New Zealand High Commissioner to dress him down, calling him something obscene. Our High Commissioner was taken aback and complained to me. I told him that proves how close the two countries are. Can you imagine an Australian minister talking to a French, Japanese or British ambassador in such terms? When Aussies and Kiwis call each other bastards, it has a different meaning.

Colonialism came late to Australasia. Several hundred years before, the Dutch had taken control of the East Indies (Indonesia), the Portuguese Timor, and the British India. Spain occupied Chile, which had a constitution more than a hundred years before the Treaty of Waitangi. The word 'posh' came from the shipping instructions of the ruling English class en route to India, who demanded the luxury berths, defined as 'port out, starboard home'. Thus they could bask in the morning sun under an empire on which the sun would never set.

Commercial interest in New Zealand came with a rush for oil. Whale oil. Australia was to be a home for criminals. (Little has changed but it's not a prerequisite for citizenship or immigration any more.) A reluctant Britain finally laid claim to New Zealand after an interest was shown by other European imperial powers. New Zealand's history, our political, economic and social developments are so similar to Australia's that we have produced citizens who are frequently mistaken for each other by outsiders, to the disgust of both. But did New Zealand miss an historic opportunity to join the Commonwealth of Australia at the turn of the century?

The pressures to form an Australian federation came to a head in the 1880s. New Zealand's delegates to a conference, Sir Frederick Whitaker and Harry Atkinson, both spoke in support of a federal council. Victoria's premier told a cheering crowd that 'no one worked more heartily towards a United Australasia than the delegates from New Zealand'. But New Zealand's House of Representatives opposed our joining and that was that.

In 1890 and 1891 further conferences were held to promote federation. New Zealand again sent delegates but non-committal MPs continued to out-number the pro-federation forces.

MPs were reluctant to see their power and prestige transferred across the Tasman. Finally in the 1890s Premier 'King' Dick Seddon kicked for touch and established a royal commission to report to Parliament. He refused to give a lead, for or against. The royal commission in due course damned the proposal in the quaint language of the day, suggesting that a new federated nation would result in a New Zealand government with the reduced powers of a state assembly. They reported that 'States, Governments, must therefore decline in power, dignity and importance'. They also argued that the public finances of New Zealand would be seriously prejudiced.

On the issue of defence the commissioners reported that 'so long as Great Britain holds command of the sea, New Zealand is quite able to undertake her own land defence'. They even suggested that New Zealand increase the annual subsidy paid to the imperial government for defence, as the colonies were uneasy about expansionist German and French moves at the time. Gun emplacements had already been erected to face down any Russian interest, one on average for every 1000 miles of coastline. No wonder the Russians were frightened off.

On every subject considered, including postal and telegraphic services, administration of justice and other departments, the social condition of the working classes and 'coloured labour', the commissioners recommended against federation. Race and climate were central considerations for New Zea-land's gentlemen legislators. New Zealand Maori had been given the vote, but Australia's Aborigines had not. Four parliamentary seats had been specifi-cally put aside for Maori in 1867. It was doubted whether Australians would even understand Treaty of Waitangi issues. Anyway, New Zealand MPs proudly claimed, the Maori were genetically superior to Aborigines.

Hansard also records MPs suggesting that Queensland's climate was no good for the white man. Captain Russell told Parliament: 'I believe that, from the difficulties in climate arose the real cause for the troubles between the people.' The member for Auckland Central said that: 'Nothing but coloured labour can colonise the northern portion of Australia.'

Sir George Grey added that the climate in northern Australia was so warm that it would be impossible for Europeans to work in the fields. Of course they could be present as directors and managers of colonised labour. He might have been right if you look at the high red-neck vote for ultra-nationalist Pauline Hanson.

New Zealand had already put special tax of £100 p.a. on Chinese workers and feared Indian and Chinese labour flooding New Zealand from Australia if there was political union. Fear of the 'yellow peril' was then common to every colonial capital. These were the days of the British empire and MPs were worried that ties with London could be weakened.

Meanwhile other MPs had shifted their focus. During one debate on federation it was suggested that instead it was the New Zealand white man's duty to form a New Zealand empire by annexing the Pacific Islands, including Hawaii. One MP even talked of taking over Argentina. New Zealand's Pacific imperialist design finally resulted in the acquisition of the Cook Islands in 1900, and later Western Samoa from the Germans during the First World War. Stout, as premier, talked of a Pacific confederation of New Zealand, Samoa, Tonga and Fiji.

Premier Richard Seddon also sought a confederation of island states centred on New Zealand, saying: 'There is always danger in delay ... any postponement would be against the best interests of this colony and the people of the Islands.' New Zealand must not 'remain quiescent, inactive, dilatory and indifferent while a great Commonwealth of Australia is being formed so close to us .... [and] stand by and allow that Commonwealth to rise up, and, like a great tree overshadow us, whilst we go on doing nothing.'

By this stage the idea of political union with Australia was doomed. Sir John Hall suggested that the 1200 miles of ocean separating the two countries were 1200 arguments against. The main electorate support had come from Southland because the major product that New Zealand could export competitively to Australia, other than timber, was oats. When Joseph Ward, later premier and still New Zealand's longest-ever serving minister, argued for federation he was accused of selling New Zealand out for a plate of porridge. Australia's and New Zealand's product mix at the time was competitive rather than complimentary.

One constructive hangover from the days of federation discussions is that at Australian ministerial meetings, where state and federal ministers meet on a regular basis to discuss issues such as transport and education, a New Zealand minister is present to contribute to the discussion. That's a unique arrangement, without any legal or constitutional standing. Where else in the world would this happen?

No New Zealand or Australian politician has seriously suggested political union for over 90 years. Australian High Court Judge Kirby is the only figure of substance I have heard raise the issue recently. I pointed out at the time that no one on either side of the Tasman would dispute that we are the best of mates, but that political union would do the opposite of what its authors intended. It would drive us apart (not to mention weaken our rugby team).

But economic integration is a different story. Experience shows that when restrictions on trade and commerce between states of comparable development are lifted, both sides prosper. This has been shown in the US and German Zollverein, where independent and quarrelling German mini-states combined in economic and political union to form the powerhouse of federal Germany. Imagine 50 separate states of America each with its own currency, commercial laws and social customs. The US didn't look inwards, it looked west, south and everywhere.

Through Closer Economic Relations (CER), New Zealand and Australia have achieved almost everything the federationists wanted in economic terms, but without sacrificing political, social or cultural independence.

New Zealand's unsung hero of CER was National minister Hugh Templeton, who had to battle Sir Robert Muldoon in the National government in the early 1980s. (After steadfastly resisting bringing the two countries together economically, Sir Robert later claimed that CER was his greatest achievement.)

As Trade Minister I was able to progress the initial agreement during the mid and late 1980s with a like-minded Labour administration in Australia. Today Australia is New Zealand's biggest market for manufactured exports and tourism, and New Zealand is Australia's most important manufacturing market and second-biggest tourism market. There are more jobs in Australia based on manufactured exports to New Zealand than from Australian exports to Japan.

CER, although widely criticised at the time and even opposed by a Labour Party conference, has been even more successful than I had imagined. Two-way trade since its inception has grown from $2 billion to $12 billion in 15 years. Everyone is winning. We were the first two countries to conclude a protocol for the services sector; it's the cleanest trade and economic arrangement anywhere outside Wales, Scotland and England, the states of America, and the provinces of Germany.

But though such economic co-operation makes perfect sense, political union is not a runner. In foreign policy and defence terms it's most unlikely that New Zealand and Australia will ever have different objectives. But we may travel to those common objectives by different roads, and will do so with more effect as separate nation states than through one voice in the UN and the other great and noble international institutions.

And occasionally we will take different roads. As New Zealand's Foreign Minister I was able to use New Zealand's naval frigates as a neutral venue for peace talks between representatives of Papua-New Guinea and Bougainville. But some Australian politicians were upset: they saw this as their sphere of influence and resented New Zealand's 'interference'. This is silly sibling rivalry. Foreign Minister Don McKinnon's patience and persistence have paid off: we now have a peace accord.

New Zealand sent peacekeepers to the Balkans; Australia did not. Australia has tens of thousands of Croatian and Serbian immigrants, some of whom have fought as mercenaries and enlisted soldiers on both sides in that region's appalling civil war. New Zealand's immigration mix is different: over 95 per cent of our migrants from the former Yugoslavia are Croatians. The split in Australia is more like 50-50. Thus we have the domestic liberty to be physically more supportive of the Dayton Accord. The doctrine of same objectives, different roads is not threatening. It doesn't weaken our collective ambitions, it strengthens them.

It's in no one's interests that Australia does badly. We need them to win. New Zealand needs a successful, prosperous Australia because jobs and security in New Zealand are strongly linked to the success of that country.

But I shocked New Zealand officials by saying once that the biggest threat to New Zealand was Australia. That is, if Australia miscalculates or fails. The nightmare for a New Zealand prime minister is a call in the middle of the night from the Australian prime minister saying, 'Gidday, mate, it's hit the fan (somewhere). Our troops are in the air, are you with us?'

The danger for New Zealand is not in being too close to Australia, but in not being close enough to influence policy formation as well as the execution of that policy in defence, trade and other external relations matters.

Warren Cooper, National's Minister of Defence, coined the phrase CDR to mean Closer Defence Relations, and co-operation between the two countries on defence issues has reached a peacetime high. The New Zealand Defence corporate plan cites 'Assisting in countering incursions in Australia' as a solemn policy objective, sanctified even by the Treasury.

Australian Defence Minister Robert Ray suggested a few years ago that the two defence forces would one day merge. But that would serve only to drive us apart. I believe they should do everything but merge: that would weaken us both. Better to follow the doctrine of the same objective, different roads. A more formal Joint Chiefs of Staff structure would be a step in the right direction.

Synergy means that one and one can equal three; combined and co-operative actions result in the sum of the two parts being greater than the whole.

We need to pursue economic integration with Australia rather than political federation: evolution not revolution. Political independence and economic strength through interdependence have served us well. There should not be any earth-shattering changes sought in the future. We need to work patiently away at the minor problems, such as the export of apples or salmon, abolishing passports to create a trans-Tasman economy and society of two independent partners, and then look further.

A common currency is a generation away because of our different product mixes. A common currency would require a joint agreement on deficits, debts and even tax. And Australians would never surrender to a deal in which New Zealand would have half the influence. Australians who talk of common currency really mean that New Zealand should adopt the Australian dollar.

But it would be timely for joint parliamentary select committees to consider joint commercial law and new legal structures in our region to replace the Privy Council. Perhaps a Pacific Privy Council that could also look to the needs of the Pacific Island nations.

In preparation for the next century, given the doctrine of 'same objectives, different roads', we need to lay down some markers.

New Zealand and Australia are regarded as part of the 'Western Europe and others' bloc in the UN. That's historically inappropriate. A new Pacific community would provide a base for more effective work, and leverage, into the power structures of ASEAN, APEC, the UN, the WTO and other international agencies. In the end, nothing that politicians – or lawyers – can do will break our bonds of affection.

Joint parliamentary select committees ought to be established as part of the security structure of the region. A leadership council of Parliamentarians from government and opposition parties from both countries would ensure that the relationship does not suffer as a result of individual parties' good or ill fortune at the polls.

New Zealand and Australia should continue their co-operation in institutions such as the UN, WTO and APEC. To create further political and economic leverage we should also begin work in the South Pacific towards a Pacific Parliament.

Sixteen years ago I published a little book entitled *A Pacific Parliament*. That was a long time ago and it's slightly embarrassing to look back on, but the fundamental proposal of a political infrastructure to unite our region to produce common values and outcomes is still relevant. I wrote that the Pacific Forum, a worthy and useful gathering of political leaders, ought to be backed up by a Pacific Parliament representing all government and opposition factions from the region, as numbers allow.

My model was the more modest Nordic Council, rather than the European Parliament. Thus MPs would be representatives in their own Parliament but also in a Pacific Parliament, which would meet for only a week or so a year in different capitals. Australia would be the strongest influence in this grouping of Parliaments, aimed at giving us collective leverage in ASEAN, APEC and ultimately the UN. We would be the Greece to their Rome.

CER is a trade treaty between economic equals. New Zealand and Australia should, in the quaint terminology of GATTspeak, be backed up by an extended SPARTECA (South Pacific Regional Trade and Economics Agreement), which already allows for a 'special and differential' relationship between the Pacific Islands and New Zealand.

It is time to reshape our political architecture across the Tasman and the Pacific to give us political and economic leverage in the wider world. I think I know how, and I believe its time has come.

CHAPTER NINE

Security and Defence: From Coercion to Persuasion

Peace is a stern moral task not a shore to be reached by simply riding on an historical wave. – Immanuel Kant, 1795.

WE LIVE IN A complicated, difficult and dangerous world – the post-Cold War age. Cold War polarisation created dangerous and deadly certainty. From Berlin to Botswana to Vanuatu and Chile the battle lines were drawn. Resources and political attention were riveted on winning the struggle for ideological and geographical supremacy. This worked to the advantage of developing countries and their powerful elites. Anything could be forgiven if the result was the containment of communism.

Along with economic globalisation we have seen the globalisation of liberal democratic and economic values. It ought to be a time of celebration. Never have so many people and nations been free. Nations that history thought had disappeared have re-emerged, along with ancient ethnic and religious rivalries and hatreds.

Western capitalism and values have triumphed for the present. The communist foe was engaged, routed and humiliated as its grotesque ideology was seen to fail at every level. Developing countries, whose anti-colonial and nationalistic impulses were seduced by Marxist anti-capitalist, anti-imperialistic theories are no longer vulnerable to this failed, godless gospel. That dangerous global chess game is over.

In a way the developing countries are now weaker. They can no longer play Washington off against Moscow or Beijing. Even some Pacific Island countries tried that 'un-diplomatic card' in the 1980s. They never really wanted Soviet or Libyan influence in their fragile economies. But it did make the United States, Australia and New Zealand sharpen their focus and increase their aid, respect and assistance.

Cynics say that is why the West is no longer motivated to help out in trouble spots in Africa. These countries will not now otherwise be 'lost' to communism. Strategic resources are safe.

Now that the Cold War is over, will there be a new – or in fact a renewal of the very old – clash between Islamic and Christian blocs? Will the future economic race be between what Lee Kwan Yew termed Confucian capitalism and Christian capitalism? Will Russia emerge as a neo-fascist economy and society like Chile in the 1970s? Will it then, like Chile, advance towards democracy?

Samuel Huntington's bestseller *The Clash of Civilizations* suggested a return to the power blocs of old, and that future clashes would be on the fault lines of cultures and civilisations: Timor, Afghanistan, the Ukraine, Turkey.

But Huntington underestimates how cultures and religions can fracture from within. There are no homogeneous Muslim or Christian or Confucian blocs. Witness the vast differences in the interpretation of Islam between Iran, Iraq and Indonesia. It was Christians who waged the 100 Years War against one another, not to mention the First and Second World Wars.

Migrants take to their new countries baggage from the past. The most enthusiastic fundraisers for the IRA have never left Boston. Money is raised for the Tamil Tigers in New Zealand and Canada. New Zealand once enjoyed a healthy Yugoslav club with Croatians and Serbs working together – until the war in that country put paid to the club's future too and it split into three clubs.

The world today is therefore less certain, more unstable. Instability causes anxiety among policymakers, for good reason. Who wants an unstable Indonesia, or a fractured and fractious China or Russia? Economic security and growth mean political stability and security. Thus APEC, WTO and CER are as important as any military alliance. We need both.

For the first 100 years after the Treaty of Waitangi, New Zealand didn't have a foreign policy. Such matters were safely left to the old hands at Whitehall. We didn't need diplomacy, we had the empire. Britannia ruled the waves. New Zealand paid millions of pounds in the 1930s to reinforce Singapore as an Asian Gibraltar. Pity we didn't insist the guns pointed the right way. Our first diplomatic post other than London was not opened until the Second World War cast doubts on Britain and the empire's capacity to protect New Zealand and our interests. We then correctly sought the support of the major Pacific power, the United States.

New Zealand has moved from being a colonial child to a stroppy adolescent and is now hopefully a mature adult. As a colonial child we sought comfort from Mother England, big brother Washington and cousin Australia. Then as a cheeky teenager we rebelled and sought more independence, a larger say in our own destiny and rejected others' apron strings. While we wanted to leave home and go flatting, we still wanted 'mother' to do some of the washing, provide a meal and the occasional loan to buy petrol.

Now as a confident young adult nation we ought to be able to consider the future with maturity, and decide what's right and wrong in terms of our own legitimate self-interest, not with a juvenile anti-American or anti-European post-colonial cringe. This new age of maturity will take new skills and sophistication, new ideas and a good-natured sense of proportion.

The defining foreign policy issues of the 1970s and 80s were the anti-nuclear and anti-apartheid campaigns. For New Zealand, the nuclear debate was not just about warheads and missiles: it was an expression of nationhood and became a celebration of our nation's uniqueness.

We've come so far today that both policies are now accepted even by many of those who were their most severe critics at the time. Foreign Minister Don McKinnon's pro-nuclear credentials back then were impeccable. He even resigned from his position as National's spokesperson on defence in protest at his party's decision to go non-nuclear. He has been consistent and principled. Recently he likened New Zealand's nuclear position to a national park, which can't be touched. It's now part of the New Zealand culture. He is correct.

International policy is more than an expression of a nation's self-interest. It is also an expression of a society's values. Our values are unashamedly liberal and democratic. We draw on the history of all the peoples who have migrated to New Zealand over the centuries.

We are a nation of immigrants. We are not just European. We are not only Asian, nor are we solely Polynesian. We are a unique blend of all these cultures. This is what gives us a special insight into the issues that drive and divide our region.

We find affinity with the anti-colonial views of developing countries. Our Irish influence and the experiences from the Scottish clearances demand it. We know of the struggle of indigenous people to preserve their cultural sovereignty. Our Treaty of Waitangi gives us a special appreciation of the ambitions of the Pacific and the sensitivities of indigenous peoples.

We have reached a stage in our development when there needs to be more depth and intellectual vigour in what passes for a debate on security and defence issues in New Zealand. It's more than whether or not we buy new frigates. If a new frigate is purchased the right will celebrate peace in our time. If no frigates are purchased, the left will celebrate a peace to end all peace. Then the defence 'debate' will be over, until the next major purchase.

We need to fashion a security response that goes beyond a frigate or two. Expenditure must be increased and our focus sharpened.

Defence is a minor but central part of national security. Most governments in our region have a powerful contingent of military representatives in their cabinets, but Minister of Defence in New Zealand is a junior position. In fact New Zealand's defence capacity is so low that we cannot, with integrity, honour our basic current treaty agreements. Our UN commitments to peacekeeping stretch our resources and endanger personnel.

Defence spending has been cut by 30 per cent since the mid-1980s. Soldiers have used their own pay to purchase boots. An army private is paid 28 per cent less than the average wage. The absence of even a modest military capacity pushes back New Zealand's ability to be part of political solutions.

We now have more police than front-line soldiers. We couldn't handle a major civil disaster. Our military are so understaffed, underfunded and underprepared that the 'line' I once used when meeting foreign leaders, that New Zealand is a threat to no one other than ourselves, may now be true.

To be sustained, military expenditure must have the support of the people and the politicians, and not just on Anzac Day. Therefore, the social and peacekeeping role of the military needs renewed focus. A chef, driver or fitter and turner with military training will always get the nod from a prospective employer ahead of private-sector trained job applicants. Why? Because they are good workers, well disciplined, and have a highly deserved reputation.

A new Ministry of External Defence, with a minister who also has responsibility for Civil Defence and civil emergency services, could provide the synergy to widen the scope and reach of the military promotion pyramid. However, we must never forget the core duties of the military; soldiers make good peacekeepers but the reverse is not always true.

Our troops, sappers and medical corps do excellent work in the Pacific Islands. Why not, once a year, set up emergency hospitals with Civil Defence involvement and do some dentistry and health checks in the poorer regions of New Zealand, such as the Far North, or the East Coast?

There is a truth about male behaviour that is preyed on by 'gangs', and which we liberals feel uncomfortable with. Some young men need, and appreciate, discipline. No one has loved them enough to tell them to turn off the TV and go to bed. Young people at risk should be given the option of military training when they are in low-level trouble. Other countries have very successful penal battalions that are worthy of study also.

However, it is good that New Zealand has one of the most sophisticated and powerful peace movements in the world. Let's hope one day all nations have similar movements of people of conscience. Such movements only exist in the countries where political leaders can be held accountable for their excesses or bad judgments.

That's why we admired so much the brave young people in Tienanmen Square and Myanmar. Let's hope there is, some day, a strong peace movement in North Korea. It puzzles me that New Zealand MPs can sign letters addressed to the leaders of South Korea complaining about the lack of trade union rights, but won't organise a similar letter to the leaders of North Korea about the carnage in that country. I was told that the stories of cannibalism and starvation in North Korea were US propaganda. When I responded that many of the stories came from North Korean refugees in China, I was told that China was a puppet of the United States. That must come as a surprise to the State Department. Someone must tell Bill and Hillary immediately.

But every Hiroshima Day the more extreme in the peace movement attack the United States for its use of atomic weapons to hasten the end of the Second World War. The grim truth is that more people would have died if the Allies had invaded Japan, or continued the bombing of Japanese cities for another year. People make the best decisions they can, given the evidence at hand. The people at Nagasaki and Hiroshima were martyred to science, but their suffering was so intense and tragic that these doomsday bombs have never been used since. That's little consolation, but what other weapon has been used only twice?

Some people are escalating an anti-nuclear message to an anti-military position. That's not isolationism, or even neutralism, it's unilateral pacifism. Many even oppose having a security intelligence service, which is any country's first line of defence. There are a substantial number of New Zealand MPs, in more than one party, who believe the Gulf War was a mistake. Yet I believe protecting 80 per cent of the world's oil was of importance, as were the inhabitants of Kuwait.

After advancing for a generation the proposition that the UN should be more proactive, the old left in New Zealand wrung their hands in dismay when the UN rallied against Saddam Hussein. One MP even claimed the war was fought for TV ratings. It was immature, anti-American, 1960s hippie double-speak. Thankfully UN Secretary General Kofi Annan ignored such shallow advice when a second war threatened.

A prominent activist phoned me complaining that on CNN a new US technology had been made public that would allow computer-guided missiles to attack Baghdad with such surgical precision that they could target specific buildings, even rooms. To his disgust, I said I thought this was great. In earlier wars the whole city would have been levelled to achieve the same result, with appalling civilian loss.

When I became Minister of Foreign Affairs I invited the Labour Party's Foreign Affairs and Defence Committee to lunch. All had been appointed to this committee: most had never been to party conferences, most had never been elected to anything inside the party, and none had been elected to any public office. All were vegetarians. They said I was out of touch and unrepresentative. I knew I had problems.

I've been told that New Zealand has no enemies, or that we couldn't defend our islands even if we poured our total GNP into defence. True, but the absence of a military capacity weakens our ability to be part of a political solution. Others gain headlines by mounting trite arguments about a supposed trade-off between hip operations and defence expenditure.

The globalisation of the world economy, the end of the Cold War and the emergence of a single superpower (the US) means the left must stop making policy by bumper sticker and the right according to the sway of opinion polls. We must beware slogans like 'positive neutrality', whatever that means. As V.K. Krishna Menon said, 'That expression "positive neutrality" is a contradiction in terms. There can no more be a positive neutrality than there can be a vegetarian tiger!'

Human evolution has seen us progress from families, to tribes, to the city state, to the nation state and now to regional economic and political interdependency through arrangements such as APEC, CER, NAFTA, the EU and SPARTECA. These economic arrangements vary in their political effectiveness, but their historic thrust is profound. Just as with the creation of a United States in North America, and the economic unification of jealous provinces to create the economic powerhouse of Germany, these new arrangements are providing economic growth, security and common political values, which is a matter of enormous economic political and military significance.

Could European Union members ever go to war again? It seems unlikely. More than 1000 years of historical rivalry and warfare have been leapfrogged by the creation of the EU, NATO, the European Parliament and a maze of other pan-European arrangements.

The identification of economic and political interests today is becoming increasingly regionalised. Over 60 per cent of New Zealand's trade goes to the Asia Pacific region. All New Zealanders' security and living standards are therefore linked to the region's economic success.

We are not an Asian nation, no matter how often former National Prime Minister Jim Bolger said we were. Asians laugh at that proposition.

We need an Austronesian grouping of Australia, New Zealand and the Pacific nations to promote our common interests. From that base we can then engage inside APEC and ASEAN within the wider Asian region.

The ASEAN Regional Forum brings together most of the countries which influence or are involved in the security of the Asia Pacific region, including the United States, China, Japan, Russia and India, as well as smaller nations such as Australia and New Zealand. The forum is an important step towards the creation of a sense of strategic community in a region where there is little history of inclusive multilateral approaches to security or defence. It also has an important role in encouraging regional support for international regimes.

Seismic changes in economic power over the last few decades place the Asia Pacific region at the centre of both opportunity and danger. The main issue is economic security. Without 3 to 5 per cent growth the economic stability and thus security of all the region's countries is threatened. That's why I have always seen APEC and GATT/WTO as vital instruments of peace and security.

So just what are the current trends within the Asia Pacific region?

Our region faces its biggest threat to stability since the Second World War. At the time of writing Indonesia was capturing the headlines. The economic crisis in Asia in recent months has hit particularly hard in Indonesia. Indonesia's currency has crashed by 75 per cent. The IMF plan originally agreed to by the Indonesian government got into trouble. Even Australian Prime Minister Howard said it was too severe. It was. How could the IMF suggest that rice subsidies be removed in one season when the currency had dropped 80 per cent, world rice prices had gone up due to shortages, and Indonesia needed to import 5 million tonnes, 40 per cent of the world's crop?

These price hikes and shortages brought about a revolutionary situation. Economic failure always does. But it is only revolutionary because there is no peaceful way to effect change. President Suharto had to go, but the fundamental economic problems will remain. Indonesia is an authoritarian society, not a totalitarian society, which needs a soft political and economic landing as it moves to a more open and democratic society.

Examine Indonesia's history. It is only recently a nation. The world's fourth-largest country, and by far the largest Muslim nation, Indonesia became independent with the charismatic Sukarno as father of the nation. After enjoying its initial liberation from colonial rule the economy came close to collapse as he indulged in major showcase investments and monuments to his fantasies.

Utilising an old political trick he diverted attention by orchestrating a threat to Indonesia's integrity by the newly created federation of Malay states, Malaysia. Singapore was then part of Malaysia, later to leave in trying but peaceful circumstances.

In polite diplomatic language we didn't call it a war, it was labelled 'confrontation'. New Zealand troops were engaged in this non-war.

Indonesia had the third-largest communist party when Marxism was at its peak in the Soviet Union and China. Marxism was a seductive idea to those nations being reborn out of their colonial bondage. Not satisfied with blaming outsiders for their economic failures, nationalist leaders blamed the ethnic Chinese merchant class.

In a perverse way, xenophobia unites the human race. Hundreds of Chinese were killed in Malaysia and hundreds of thousands were slaughtered in Indonesia. General Suharto toppled Sukarno in a bloody coup and went on to create dynamic and successful economic growth. Average incomes in Indonesia increased more than fivefold under his leadership. They even successfully invented a new language to unite their many peoples.

China is the rising star in the region. Its population is double that of the US and Europe combined. China will have an economy equal to the US within a generation and stronger than the US and Japan put together within a lifetime. Some 28 per cent of the world's cranes are at work in one city – Shanghai. They pour more concrete in China in two months than we have in 150 years. China is building several hundred deep-water fishing boats designed for the Antarctic fisheries.

China's maturity as a front-line nation that seeks to co-operate and compete in the world has been reinforced by its leaders' strong decision not to devalue the currency to maintain competitiveness as regional currencies slid and crashed. So far, so good.

The containment theories advanced by belligerent 'hawks' in the US and elsewhere are wrong, dangerous and reactionary. We need to welcome China into the world community, and eventually into the WTO within the discipline of its rules. If China's growth stalls then our markets shrink, not only in China, but in the many nations in our region whose growth and stability is now linked to China's.

Napoleon once said, 'China is a giant – let her sleep.' But that's not an option. Indeed, the growth, stability and security of our region hinge on China's success, not her isolation.

However, there are uneasy political implications in all this. China's history suggests that unity and cohesion will always be more important than the Western values of democracy and human rights. China has moved from a totalitarian society to more of an authoritarian society along the lines of others in the region – the old tiger is being born again alongside the young tigers of our region.

There are 50 million overseas Chinese, the greatest of the global tribes. They dominate most South East Asian economies. Their very success makes them vulnerable – they are the Jews of Asia. The largest armies in history massed alongside the Soviet-Sino border fewer than 15 years ago. There are up to 5 million Chinese, many illegal immigrants, in Siberia, compared with 7 million Russians. If overseas Chinese face the genocide they have in the past, will China be silent? For the first time in a thousand years China now has a blue-water navy capable of protecting her interests.

Asia is not a particularly comfortable region. Currently there is military build-up in Asia – even a nuclear race – while the rest of the world is cutting military budgets.

Japan is the world's second-strongest economy. In effective terms it now has the world's second most powerful military machine. Since 1946 its constitution has enforced a 1 per cent of GNP limit on defence spending, but 1 per cent of its 1997 GNP is quite a sum. At the Kennedy round of GATT negotiations it was said that this would assist Japan and other developing countries.

The Japanese coastguard recently headed off a flotilla of protesters from Hong Kong and Taiwan headed for the Serkaku Islands, which are halfway between Taiwan and Okinawa. Japan has since 1905 laid claim to rocky islets claimed by South Korea. Korea's claim goes back 1400 years. In the 1980s a Korean pop song, 'Tokdo is Our Land', so inflamed popular opinion the government banned it.

The Korean peninsula, with both sides heavily armed, continues to threaten regional and world stability. North Korea's leadership is erratic, even certifiable. Further deterioration of North Korea's economy could lead to a crisis in that country involving a high humanitarian cost and requiring external assistance. It can only be hoped that this will hasten the peaceful reunification of the two Koreas. Reunification in turn would have implications for Korea's economic growth and for the strategic outlook in the region.

The world's response to the Asian economic crisis has been supportive, but if the economic fallout spreads to Japan and China, then we have a timebomb on our doorstep, with serious security implications for New Zealand and our region. Some 40 per cent of China's loans are underperforming, a property bubble sits waiting to explode. Millions of workers will be sacked from state-owned enterprises that are consuming more than half of the nation's budget because of their inefficiencies and losses, stealing investment in real jobs, health and education. Sound familiar to any New Zealanders?

In the past New Zealand has prided itself on its independent thinking in foreign policy terms. But an independent foreign policy cannot be isolationist. A mature policy of independent, enlightened regional self-interest is quite the opposite. I oppose the principle of 'neutralism' in international policy. How can we be neutral to the great global events of our age? Could we be neutral to the agony in Cambodia, or to the terror and horror in Africa?

While an independent foreign policy is a laudable principle, we live in an interdependent world. Everything we do has an impact on our neighbours, just as their actions affect us. Small nations need international rules of behaviour not only for collective security, but also for collective development and environmental survival.

New epochs demand new responses. Instead of saying 'Yankee go home' or 'Japan stay home' we should say the opposite. Let's keep things in perspective and keep a keen sense of humour about our place in the scheme of things. George Schultz, the US Secretary of State at the time of our nuclear differences, published a 1000-page autobiography that didn't mention New Zealand once. Australia was worthy of only one sentence and that was about a meeting of the author with Bob Hawke before either was in politics.

Lee Kwan Yew was once asked by a New Zealand interviewer why, if he admitted that Singapore had no enemies, he welcomed the US fleet. 'It's because we have the US fleet that we have no enemies,' he sweetly replied. It's exactly because we can never defend our interests and our islands alone that we seek constructive collective security, throughout the UN and other arrangements.

We need to make our region more interdependent to bind us together by self-interest. My doctrine of independence through interdependence, leverage through engagement, represents the view that international arrangements, treaties and institutions advance the interests and independence of the sovereign state.

Small nations like New Zealand don't have power, but they can have influence. Few nations have a better or more respected role in international peacekeeping than New Zealand. New Zealand troops and police have been involved successfully in the Balkans, Cyprus, Sinai, the Gulf, Cambodia, Africa and Haiti. We train mine-detector teams in many tragic locations. No nation has sailed, marched and flown further to fight for peace and to keep it. Our political proposals are given strength and credibility because they stand on the sturdy shoulders and reputations of our competent military servicemen and women.

Terence O'Brien, director of the Centre for Strategic Studies at Victoria University of Wellington, suggested in an address in April 1998 that the facilitation role New Zealand played in formulating a solution to the Bougainville crisis could be repeated in other parts of the world.

> The qualifications for facilitator that New Zealand ... possesses reside in the fact that it has no grand strategic design or hidden external agenda. Its non-threatening stature, coupled with a capacity for objectivity and for problem-solving, provide the basic sinews for its role in the case of Bougainville. No other country in the neighbourhood is quite as well endowed. These are assets in today's world, given the nature of conflict and instability, especially when ethnic and other particularist differences are involved ...
>
> Successive New Zealand governments have proved diffident, however, about employing or applying such assets in ways like, say, Norway, a country of comparable size and world view.

Peter Fraser led the charge for small nations when the UN was formed. There is a leadership vacuum internationally that New Zealand could fill with modesty, vigour and integrity. Alas, at the moment we lack the leadership and the vision.

Economic nationalism often escalates to military nationalism. The government of India was elected on a slogan of 'Yes to McChips but No to McDonald's'. They argued for investment in technology, but not for fast foods and banking.

The recent nuclear testing in India received 90 per cent popular support in that country. People saw it as a sign that their nation was assuming its place among the superpowers. Very phallic. Pakistan responded and a race is on. But most likely is that now that they both have their bombs, both will sign up to the Comprehensive Test Ban Treaty. They are in the top 'club'. The idea of an Islamic bomb shatters what supporters claim was a monopoly on nuclear weapons by the imperialist powers.

The technological reality is that nations can test weapons now by computer simulation. It's cheaper, cleaner, more secret and possibly even more dangerous because public opinion cannot be alerted to these dangers. Our foreign affairs, security service and defence personnel continue to co-operate, and desperately need to, over the grim prospects of terrorists obtaining nuclear weapons and nuclear waste. The technology is relatively simple and the black market exists.

The danger is that military/industrial complex will take over and become a force in itself, then try to fund the programme it seeks to export the nuclear technology. For peaceful purposes, of course. That's what the existing nuclear powers say. India did not sign the Test Ban Treaty, accusing the existing nuclear powers of wanting to maintain their monopoly in this deadly and dreadful technology. India is a superpower. But then Brazil could claim the same …

Now despite recent events in India and Pakistan, the trend throughout the world in regard to nuclear weapons is overwhelmingly positive. The number of nuclear weapons and storage sites round the world has fallen dramatically since end of the Cold War. The Washington-based Natural Resources Defence Council has estimated that the five declared nuclear powers deployed about 36,000 nuclear weapons at the end of 1997, down from nearly 70,000 in the mid-1980s.

The warheads are housed at an estimated 142 sites in 11 countries, which the council says represents a fivefold decrease in less than a decade. And the numbers are expected to continue shrinking as the United States and Russia retire older weapons under Strategic Arms Reduction treaties. Nuclear weapons are no longer stored in South Korea, Guam, Bulgaria, Hungary, Poland, the former East Germany or Czechoslovakia, nor in 14 former Soviet republics.

The United States has collected nuclear waste from former enemies and flown it back home for disposal. It is the only nation capable of such action and it makes for a safer world. The US has also assisted in dismantling nuclear weapons in Russia, Belarus, Kazakstan and the Ukraine, at considerable cost to their taxpayers. Someone, somewhere, ought to say thank you. We whinge when a ship carrying nuclear waste sails within 1000 miles of us. So we should, but then as Willy Brandt once told me: 'Idealism increases in direct proportion to your distance from the problem.'

The European Union and United States were generous in aid to what was the Soviet Union at the time of the nuclear disaster at Chernobyl. The clean-up still consumes 12 per cent of the Ukrainian budget.

With the collapse of the Soviet Union, the nuclear situation became even more dangerous as nuclear weapons were stationed in many new states that were politically unstable. By patient negotiation, that risk was covered and brave action by presidents Yeltsin and Clinton detargetted nuclear missiles. President Clinton also took US nuclear forces off alert.

Praise ought to be given to Japan, South Korea and the United States as the leaders who established the Korean Peninsula Energy Development Organisation, whose purpose is to negotiate the dismantling of the DPRK's nuclear programme and her capacity to develop nuclear weapons. The cost $6 to 7 billion. New Zealand and Australia have contributed prudent sums.

There is not enough money in the world to clean up the nuclear waste industry, despite generous contributions by the US and others. According to CNN in June 1998, the US alone has 25 billion gallons of nuclear waste and there's enough waste in Russia and the former Soviet republics to build 40,000 nuclear bombs.

A Chemical Weapons Convention has been signed by 100 nations. Both Russia and the US are committed to destroying their stockpiles. The Biological Weapons Convention compliance provisions are being strengthened, although, alas, Iraq stands aside. There is now an Anti-Personnel Land Mine Treaty, from which China and the US stand aside for the moment.

Conventional arms control is a more difficult matter, although in Europe, confidence and security-building measures have seen the Conventional Armed Forces in Europe Treaty eliminate 51,300 tanks, artillery pieces and combat aircraft. There have been nearly 3000 on-site inspections.

The Gulf War was different. It saved the Kuwaitis from a fate worse than the Kurds, and 80 per cent of the world's oil reserves were saved from the hands of a terrorist leader. But it also encouraged US President George Bush to announce what he called a 'new world order'. This 'war' had been fronted by the UN, acting in strict accordance with its rules and a US-led UN force, supported by the Soviets and even Islamic nations. (At the time of writing, Saddam Hussein was still in power, but the world's oil was safe.)

President Bush's new world order held out a promise that this would be the century of persuasion, unlike the last century which was one of imperialist coercion. A time when nations through democracies at home, and an international web of treaties and institutions, would advance their interests and settle their differences in a more democratic and civilised manner.

Let's hope we have learnt the grim lesson of history: we co-operate and engage or suffer the consequences.

I'm optimistic, because failure carries too much risk.

CHAPTER TEN

National Sovereignty Meets Cultural Sovereignty

THE INDIVIDUAL NATION is the basic unit in the community of nations, just as the family is the basic unit in domestic society.

The purpose of internationalism ought to be to strengthen, protect and further the rights of peoples and the nation state, not to replace it. But one issue that will see seismic division in the next century will be the fight for the right to self-determination by various indigenous peoples as the tectonic plates of race and cultures grind together.

We must give thought to the possibility that clashes in the future may be between cultures and civilisations, rather than nations, inside countries as much as outside them.

Most of the world's boundaries – from Africa to the Middle East, the Pacific and South America – have been rewritten several times this century, but cultural boundaries have not. When the Austro-Hungarians went to war the order to mobilise went out in 15 languages. Cultures and civilisations have, and will, endure forever, despite the will of generals and statesmen.

The last 50 years have seen over 100 new member states join the United Nations, many of them ancient nations that history thought had perished. Most wars of the past decade have been internal. The majority of refugees are now internal within their own nations' boundaries.

Much of our recent international law was established to cope with the decolonisation period and the retreat of the European empires. The last European empire, the Soviet Union, lasted after most others, bound by the dogma and bayonets of Marxism. The patriarchs and tsars had earlier also held their people in bondage, bound by an idea of themselves as the third Rome. Decolonisation is almost over now that the last empire has retreated home to Russia.

But colonisation was not a 'white' European invention. Cultural and tribal colonisation existed long before nations' boundaries were drawn. Minority groups and weaker tribes have had problems of domination by stronger groups since long before the age of European conquest and expansion.

The historic demons of racial injustice plague all the lands colonised by strong elements. New Zealand is not alone; indeed, our problems are small compared with those of some countries. We have the Treaty of Waitangi, which at least puts in place a legal process to resolve these problems. They wish they had such a mechanism in the Middle East, Sri Lanka and along other racial and cultural fault lines. If we didn't have a Treaty of Waitangi process, we would have to invent it. Countries without such a process fall back on common law, and now increasingly a growing body of international law as well, or they suffer ethnic violence. Indigenous rights exist with or without a treaty – look at Canada, the US and Australia.

The bloody war in the former Yugoslavia epitomises such wars from times past. Said the *Economist* in 1991:

> Yugoslavia has brought civil war back to Europe for the first time since Greece was rent in the 1940s and republicans fought fascism in Spain in the 1930s. Yugoslavia's may well be the war of the future; one waged between different tribes, harbouring centuries-old grudges about language, religion and territory, and provoking bitterness for generations to come. In their details, conflicts like these vary from place to place. The tribes may want to dominate each other, to escape each other's clutches, or merely to kill each other. But the main ingredient is the same: visceral hatred of the neighbours.

Will the world ever 'grow out of it'? Not according to US academic James Q. Wilson in *The Moral Sense*:

> What makes Serbs, Croats, Slovaks, Tosks, Armenians, Kurds, Bantus, Masai, Kikuyus, Ibos, Germans, and countless – literally countless – other peoples argue, fight, and die for 'ethnic self-determination'? Why do they seek to be ruled by 'one's own kind' when what constitutes 'one's own kind' is so uncertain and changeable, being variously defined as people whom you think are like you in language, customs, place or origin, and perhaps other, inexpressible, things as well? ... For some reason, the need for affiliation is so powerful that it reaches as far as one can find a historically plausible and emotionally satisfying principle of similarity.
>
> Erecting walls that separate 'us' from 'them' is a necessary correlate of morality since it defines that scope within which sympathy, fairness and duty operate. The chief wall is the family/clan/village, but during certain historical periods ethnicity [an abstract family, clan, or village] defines the wall.
>
> The great achievement of Western culture since the Enlightenment is to make many of us peer over the wall and grant some respect to people out-

side it; the great failure of Western culture is to deny that walls are inevitable or important.

It's difficult to have heroes when you are in your late forties, but I still have one – Senator Daniel Patrick Moynihan, who constantly commits the greatest political sin of all, namely being right too soon. He foresaw the breakup of the Soviet Union in the late 1970s and the reasons for that empire's demise. Henry Kissinger was moved to confess that Moynihan's crystal ball was more accurate than his.

Moynihan wrote an important book, called *Pandaemonium*, after Satan's capital in Milton's *Paradise Lost*, in which he said:

> If the forces of nationalism and self-determination and indigenous rights and of sovereignty are on the throne today, it is by merit: they are responses to real problems and to the experience of imperial arrangements.

Moynihan's title perfectly represents the ambivalent nature of problem. An ambivalence that is exploited by populists and ultra-nationalists, and by extremists like Pauline Hanson, who are against the MAI, the UN and indigenous rights because they claim they compromise democracy. They are attractive to the powerless and those marginalised.

Alas, most wars have been caused by politicians and leaders arguing for self-determination. Hitler claimed to be simply reuniting the Germanic people throughout Austria, Czechoslovakia and Poland. The assassination of Crown Prince Franz Ferdinand in Sarajevo in 1914 was supposedly to further the independence of the Balkans. The shot still echoes around the world. On the other side, the Allies were also fighting for democracy and self-determination. In the past God has been on all sides: war is a subjective business. Now it's democracy and self-determination. Winston Churchill's calls for democracy stopped at the edges of Europe. He certainly didn't include India. Three great Gandhis were murdered in the name of self-determination and indigenous rights.

If such divisions are inevitable, then the response of a civilised world must be to construct the means to resolve such cultural and ethnic differences peacefully.

Moynihan's *Pandaemonium* has influenced me because of its historic warning on this complex issue:

> I would like to sound a note of normative caution on the role of ethnicity in politics. The upsurge of ethnicity is a cultural gain in that it allows indi-

viduals whose identities have been submerged, or whose status has been denigrated, to assert a sense of pride in what they regard as their own. In equal measure, it is a means for disadvantaged groups to claim a set of rights and privileges which the existing powers structures have denied them.

Yet if one looks down the deep ravines of history, one sees that men in social groups need some other group to hate. The strength of primordial attachment is that emotional cohesion derives not only from some inner 'consciousness of kind', but from some external definition of an adversary as well. Where there are *Gemeinde*, there are also *Fremde*. And such divisions, when translated into politics, become, like a civil war, *parlance d'outrance*.

It was once hoped that the politics of ideology might be replaced by the politics of civility, in which men would learn to live in negotiated peace. To replace the politics of ideology with the politics of ethnicity might only be the continuation of war by other means. And those are the drawbacks of ethnicity as well.

Extreme nationalism has done more to destroy indigenous peoples and cultures than any other idea. Colonisation and imperialism were just an extension of the nationalist sentiment.

Nationalism began as a popular movement against privilege, dynastic power and empire. It was the Jacobean view, derived from Rousseau, endorsed by liberals such as John Stuart Mill and given life in a burst of 'idealism' by Woodrow Wilson and practical meaning by Franklin D. Roosevelt at Yalta. States were often created from an orgy of anti-colonialism and a drive for self-determination. Frequently without cohesion, because nationalism is about the absence of states as well as their existence.

As predicted, this nationalism based on the principles of sovereignty has take a vicious turn, from Rwanda to Yugoslavia. Twenty million Russians from the Baltic to the Black Sea are uneasy citizens in these newly emerging ancient nations. Policymakers shudder at the thought of their becoming hostage to a new wave of nationalism in the future.

The call for the legal right of all peoples to self-determination brought the US Congress to its feet in ecstatic applause when President Wilson first proposed it as one of his 14 principles. Later the UN put pen to paper in the 1960 Declaration of Independence to Colonial Countries and Peoples:

> All peoples have the right to self-determination; by virtue of that right they freely determine their political status and fully pursue their economic, social and cultural development.

In 1966 the International Covenants on Human Rights called upon member states to 'promote the realisation of the right of self-determination and [shall] respect that right in conformity with the provisions of the Charter of the United Nations'.

So just what is self-determination? Says Malcolm N. Shaw:

The principle of self-determination provides that the people of the colonially defined territorial unit in question may freely determine their own political status. Such determination may result in independence, integration with a neighbouring state, free association with an independent state or any other political status freely decided upon by the people concerned.[1]

Oh dear – a recipe for chaos, surely? Then UN Secretary General Boutros Boutros-Ghali's paper, *An Agenda for Peace*, spelled out the problem in 1992:

The United Nations has not closed its door. Yet if every ethnic, religious or linguistic group claimed statehood, there would be no limit to fragmentation, and peace, security and economic well-being for all would become ever more difficult to achieve.

Boutros-Ghali saw the solution in an increased commitment by the UN and member states to looking seriously at recognition of the rights of minority groups and cultures. This, he hoped, would allow the resolution of difficulties and conflicts in a manner that did not result in the creation of hundreds more separate nation states.

One requirement for solutions to these problems lies in commitment to human rights with a special sensitivity to those of minorities, whether ethnic, religious, social or linguistic ... The General Assembly soon will have before it a declaration on the rights of minorities. That instrument, together with the increasingly effective machinery of the United Nations dealing with human rights, should enhance the situation of minorities as well as the stability of states ...

The sovereignty, territorial integrity and independence of states within the established international system, and the principle of self-determination for peoples, both of great value and importance, must not be permitted to work against each other in the period ahead.[2]

The Secretary General's words clearly identify a central problem of the post-Cold War world. In so doing they point to the urgent need for serious and intelligent international debate about ethnicity, nationalism and self-determination. That's why after more than a decade of discussion the UN Declaration on Indigenous Rights is still not in a shape to go forward to the

General Assembly for confirmation. It won't be for another decade – and that's an optimistic outlook. After 13 years only two articles have been agreed. These are the simplest ones, suggesting that indigenous peoples have rights to a nationality, and that their rights are to be guaranteed regardless of gender.

Does the right to self-determination of a minority group have to cost the sovereignty of the nation state? Of course not: we are smarter than that. Power-sharing, devolution, federalism and constitutional guarantees of rights have been the road to social cohesion in other lands faced with these dilemmas. There are differences between minority rights, ethnic rights and indigenous rights.

The most feared word in the diplomatic dictionary is secession. The Organisation of African Unity made an interesting and profound policy statement on its foundation. It was that existing political national boundaries would stand, despite their arrogant colonial inconsistency and compromises drafted for them in foreign capitals. They knew that if the issue were opened for debate it would lead to internal dissension and civil war, and then they would be able to talk about and do nothing else. Advice the rest of the world should consider.

President Abraham Lincoln's inauguration speech has a chilling relevance for us today and echoes a warning down the ages. Imagine: here was the great man facing half his Congress who are trying to form a new confederacy, a new nation. He was looking down the barrel of civil war.

> Before entering upon so grave a matter as the destruction of our national fabric, with all its benefits, its memories, and its hopes, would it not be wise to ascertain precisely why we do it? Will you hazard so desperate a step while there is any possibility that any portion of the ills you fly from have no real existence? Will you, while the certain ills you fly to are greater than all the real ones you fly from, will you risk the commission of so fearful a mistake?
>
> From questions of this class spring all our constitutional controversies, and we divide upon them into majorities and minorities. If the minority will not acquiesce, the majority must, or the Government must cease. There is no other alternative, for continuing the Government is acquiescence on one side or the other. If a minority in such case will secede rather than acquiesce, they make a precedent which in turn will divide and ruin them, for a minority of their own will secede from them whenever a majority refuses to be controlled by such minority. For instance, why may not any portion of a new confederacy a year or two hence arbitrarily secede again,

precisely as portions of the present Union now claim to secede from it? All who cherish disunion sentiments are now being educated to the exact temper of doing this.

Is there such perfect identity of interests among the States to compose a new union as to produce harmony only and prevent renewed secession?

Plainly the central idea of secession is the essence of anarchy. A majority held in restraint by constitutional checks and limitations, and always changing easily with deliberate changes of popular opinions and sentiments, is the only true sovereign of a free people. Whoever rejects it does of necessity fly to anarchy or to despotism. Unanimity is impossible. The rule of a minority, as a permanent arrangement, is wholly inadmissible, so that, rejecting the majority principle, anarchy or despotism in some form is all that is left.

Lincoln closed his speech by saying:

We are not enemies, but friends. We must not be enemies. Though passion may have strained it must not break our bonds of affection. The mystic chords of memory stretching from every battlefield and patriot grave to every living heart and hearthstone all over this broad land, will yet swell the chorus of the Union, when again touched, as surely they will be, by the better angels of our nature.

The better angels of our nature occasionally win through. Look at the new Fijian and South African constitutions, which have arisen from the hatred of racial violence to bind these nations together.

Other leaders around the world have echoed similar sentiments. Sir Apirana Ngata and Sir Peter Buck, two eminent Maori political leaders and thinkers earlier this century, have expressed the same disdain for extreme tribalism alongside a commitment to the people in the wider sense and a vision of the future. They saved their people and their culture from extinction. Sir Peter Buck in his book *Vikings of the Sunrise* (1938) noted:

That the mixing of the Maori and European races in New Zealand inevitably will go on to the final evolution of a still more distinctive New Zealander. Where the mixing of the races now going on will end I do not know. But this mixing does not matter so long as the Maoris of today value the culture and traditions of their race and let them act as stimuli to further endeavour. In the future I see the development of a fine race of New Zealanders composed of the European and Maori.

In a powerful address Sir Peter spoke of the Maori's equality with the Europeans:

Yes, you are equal, but you have to work, work, work to prove it. It is no use you talking about illustrious ancestors and the great voyages made by the early navigators. The Maori must work with and go forward with the Pakeha so that both together could be classed under the one title of New Zealanders.

New Zealand is a young nation in many ways. Our people reflect many waves of migration. We were all boat people at one time. The first migrants who arrived 1000 or more years ago in their waka and those who arrived 1000 hours ago must each enjoy equal rights under the law as New Zealanders. Of course the first people must always have a special place.

Our collective memories also reflect the English with their history of respect for institutions and law, the agony of the Irish and their experience as the first colony of England, the Welsh, Scots, Croatians, Indians, Dutch and Chinese, who were treated so badly last century, and the new arrivals from Asia and the Pacific.

All make up the unique personality that is evolving as a distinctly New Zealand character. We are not the same, but we are equal. The Magna Carta, the Ten Commandments, the Bill of Rights, the Declaration of Independence and the Treaty of Waitangi are all part of a collective heritage.

No one came to New Zealand without a memory. It is those memories, and our experience of building a new nation, that make us what we are. We are all equal, but we are not the same. We are unique, but not alone. We share the universal truths of other cultures: history and ideas don't stop at the legal border of any nation. We are at the centre of a worldwide debate on human rights, minority sovereignty and self-determination. We can be leaders.

I believe that to date New Zealand – even South Africa, the US, Canada, and Australia – represent the best and most civilised approaches to the healing of racial injustice. Never good enough, of course: imperfect, but going the right way. If on a scale New Zealand is among the best, then Rwanda, and the former Yugoslavia, represent the worst kind of response to ethnic and indigenous differences.

How New Zealand handles the issue of the call for Maori sovereignty will shape our future. There is tremendous goodwill on both sides as we walk on eggshells to avoid the pitfalls and landmines. In fact our progress with the Treaty of Waitangi process and our history thus far give us credentials that will be an undoubted advantage in foreign policy terms. This will be an unplanned, but useful, spin-off from the treaty process.

But there is a danger here. New Zealanders have always been smug about race relations: we never had the slavery of America, nor the genocide of Australia. New Zealanders now recognise that though there is much to be proud of, there is much injustice still to heal. The New Zealand treaty process still has a long way to go.

Canada and Australia are having to face up to their historic ghosts and demons through common law and local courts because law exists now, it's not a recent creation. They have no reference point as New Zealand has with its Treaty of Waitangi; they wish they did.

Indigenous Canadians enjoyed a legal breakthrough in 1997, as *Time* magazine reported:

> For the past three decades, as Canada's native peoples tried through the courts to gain title to land their ancestors had occupied for centuries, they ran into a legal wall. Western judicial culture demanded paper trails; in many cases, native cultures lacked formal written records.
>
> Touchstones of native history, from oral traditions to linguistic and archaeological evidence, were dismissed by the courts as no substitute for documentation. If there was no formal treaty to back the claims, 'it's as if we didn't exist,' said Phil Fontaine, grand chief of the aboriginal umbrella organisation the Assembly of First Nations. In years of negotiations over disputed non-treaty lands, which could amount to more than 15 per cent of national territory, provincial and federal negotiators consistently held the upper hand.
>
> Not any more. In a unanimous decision, Canada's Supreme Court not only declared that such aboriginal title exists and is protected under the country's constitution, but also ruled that in considering the claims, governments need to respect native tradition and history as evidence.
>
> Once established, the court added, aboriginal title permits native peoples to enjoy full use of the land, including mineral and timber rights. 'It's a stunning decision and long overdue,' said Brian Slattery, a constitutional law expert at Toronto's Osgoode Hall law school. 'Now when native people go to the bargaining table they will have a whole lot more chips. For the first time they will be good as equals.'

Australia is being forced to face its hidden and shameful history in similar court actions. New Zealand provided separate parliamentary representation for Maori in 1867 but it took another 100 years for the Australian Constitution to enshrine full political rights for Australian Aborigines.

The *Bulletin* explained the Australian dilemma:

> Before the High Court decided the Mabo case it was accepted that Australia

was settled rather than conquered by the British, and that it was unoccupied and without laws – in the legal sense *terra nullus*. On British settlement, the legal and beneficial ownership of all the land was vested in the Crown, with no concept of Aboriginal law or native title being recognised.

This settled state of affairs was turned on its head by the High Court's decision in the Mabo case, in which the Meriam people claimed they had land rights over the Murray Islands in Torres Strait, and that the Crown's sovereignty over the islands was subject to the Meriams' native title to that land. After a long legal odyssey, the matter was decided by the High Court in 1992. In its landmark judgment the court abolished the doctrine of *terra nullus*, ruling that the common law of Australia recognised native title and that it must co-exist with the rights and interests of Aborigines.

In a 6:1 majority decision, the High Court found that:

- The Meriam people were entitled to possession, occupation, use and enjoyment of the Murray Islands;
- Aboriginal or native title was recognised by the common law of Australia;
- Native title was capable of extinguishment by the valid exercise of government powers; and
- Native title reflected Aborigines' entitlement to their traditional lands in accordance with their laws or customs.

In response to the Mabo judgment and its far-reaching implications for land tenure, the Liberal government of Paul Keating passed the Native Title Act, giving legislative sanction to the High Court's judgment. The main points were:

- Recognition and protection of native title
- Validation of past acts that the existence of native title had made invalid;
- Establishment of a mechanism for determining native title claims and
- Establishment of ways in which future dealings affecting native title could proceed.

The NTA defines 'native title' as the rights and interests that Aborigines and Torres Strait Islanders have in land, or water, in accordance with their traditional laws and customs. The NTA also requires that native title claimants have, under their laws and customs, a 'connection' with the land, or water. It is still not clear just how close this connection must be.

These negotiated and legislated outcomes are far superior to the use of violence and hatred that surrounds the pursuit of self-determination in some other lands.

No matter how many times I hear Martin Luther King's famous speech calling for equal rights I still get goosebumps. He is part of my generation's life; he inspired me and still does. He spoke of his dreams about the equality of all God's children:

I have a dream today.

Let freedom ring.

Let freedom ring from every village and every hamlet, from every side and city, we will be able to speed up that day, when all God's children – black men, and white men, Jews and Gentiles, Protestants and Catholics – will be able to join hands and sing in the words of that old Negro spiritual, 'Free at last, free at last, thank God Almighty, we are free at last.'

Those words echoed around the US and around the world. The words freedom and equality provoked images that both shamed and inspired a nation. These were no ordinary words; he was no ordinary man. His inspiration was touched by Lincoln's 'better angels' of our nature.

Inclusive is the opposite of exclusive; open is the opposite of closed; love is the opposite of hate. Everyone is special, but no race, religion or political system is superior. Democracy is the opposite of fascism and Marxism. There is no super-race.

No one's a racist, or worries about the colour of the doctor's skin or what country produced a vaccine, when their children are sick or need a blood transfusion. The stakes are too high: prejudice evaporates.

The civilised answer to such problems of hatred and division is to build a body of domestic and international policies, precedents, law and practices and institutions to deliver a more just outcome.

The international indigenous rights movement has many virtues and deserves support. But generalising to argue the case in every situation and nation points up the inherent dangers. A Scots Parliament represents a region, a history and geography, but nobody would suggest that a Scottish enclave in London or an Irish enclave in Liverpool should be a separate political constituency.

There are more Jews in New York than in Israel – they are a significant source of political investment and encouragement to that nation – but surely no one would suggest the establishment of a Jewish state in New York? Think about the immigrant Irish and Chinese throughout the world. What kind of chaos would ensue if some of these groups began to claim the right to self-determination in the country of their choice?

Words can mean different things to different peoples. The word 'nation' as used in the North American term 'Indian nation' means something different to what it means in Australia or New Zealand. Native American land has its own by-laws and is not subject to state law, but is answerable to federal law. So they might call it the Indian nation, but it's not a nation in the sense we would mean. Yet there is a large measure of cultural self-determination involved. Which brings us to 'sovereignty'. Just what does sovereignty mean? Does it mean political self-rule for every minority group in every country?

That's what it means for some Maori nationalists in New Zealand who have called for non-Maori New Zealanders to leave their country. Even those who have been in New Zealand for generations. That's an impossibility – go where? It's as silly and as impracticable as suggesting that Maoris with non-Maori blood export that part of them offshore. It won't happen.

What is partnership? Surely partnership cannot mean a group is entitled to 50 per cent of education expenditure, or half of the political representation?

Some people, among them some members of Parliament, are seeking an indigenous people's Parliament. They call other New Zealanders tuahiwi (foreigners). That insult is itself a breach of the Treaty of Waitangi, which guarantees non-Maori as well as Maori their rights and place.

My good friend Andrew Vercoe, of Waikato University, is certainly no extremist or racist but in his recent book *Educating Jake* he argues for separate Parliaments in New Zealand based on race to empower Maori.

Simon Reeves's book *To Honour the Treaty*, now in its second edition, in arguing for equal seats, makes the legal case that partnership under the Treaty of Waitangi means equal political representation for Maori and non-Maori. What happened to one person, one vote? Equality? Apartheid?

Most societies have small groups of extreme nationalists. I have met them in Israel, Iran, Indonesia, Malaysia and Germany, so why should New Zealand be any different? But the danger in New Zealand is that under our MMP parliamentary system they can have influence beyond their numbers. It's okay, the tail wagging the dog under MMP. But sometimes it's what's under the tail that wags the dog!

The nation state is everywhere under siege by tribal impulses. In one week in 1997 a group took over the Venice town hall and declared an independent Venice. An extremist group of right-wing militia declared an independent Texas, and Maori activists opened a Maori embassy on the East Coast of the North Island of New Zealand.

Under the guise of the language of the UN and Woodrow Wilson, a powerful worldwide movement is gathering political momentum. Groups as diverse as New Zealand Maori, the Samis of Scandinavia, the Miskito of Central America and the Aborigines of Australia have secured rights beyond their governments' authority to speak with their own voice in international forums.

This is a good thing; it's not a conspiracy but an awakening as indigenous people network and find common cause. Why shouldn't they? Everything else has become internationalised. They represent the failure of the global economy and the nation state to satisfy their physical, cultural and emotional needs.

Their position is unique legally as they are not representatives of their governments, nor of the majority of their countries' people. The traditional principle that only 'states' have standing under international law no longer applies. They challenge the legal concept of human rights being individualist by their collective approach to rights. They foster the recognition of the various rights of indigenous people under international and domestic law and have found themselves an international stage on which to do it.

It's good that some of the world's most powerless peoples are uniting in solidarity to seek redress and a voice through negotiation and law. And yet the situation is fraught with problems as the most mischievous and extreme among these groups argue that self-determination and sovereignty mean separate governments, a separate state.

In a democracy such a tiny percentage of extremists is not a problem. In non-democratic societies of course they could take power by force. Iraq today, Germany yesterday.

Moynihan's *Pandaemonium* provides this profound thought:

Freud once remarked that we pass from group psychology to individual psychology. The former is prior not only in historical but in psychological time as well. The first and basic group is the family. In political terms, the first unit was the tribe, because it was built on the basis of family. With the disintegration of the tribe, other dependency structures appeared. Nationalism is potent because it recapitulates psychologically the family structure. There is authority for protection and there is identification and warmth.

Where one seeks to pose class against nationalism, the failure to find elements of pride on the part of class allegiance is a strong handicap. Sometimes messianic hope can substitute for pride, as it did among the European working class. In large part today, that hope is forlorn. Where class appeal is united with nationalism, directing the antiplutocratic feeling against a national outsider, as Hitler did, the result is the creation of an internally cohesive movement.

Great injustice, even genocide, is an historic fact. Indigenous people's rights are at the top of the agenda at the UN and other international agencies. This is good, and inevitable. We must not be afraid of the future; we must trust and have faith in the people.

But clearly the international community could do with fresh domestic and international legal architectures to cope. Work towards this has been under way for some time.

In 1982 a Working Group on Indigenous Populations was established amid a flurry of activity at the United Nations to try to draw up a draft Declaration on the Rights of Indigenous People.

But this working group has its work cut out for it because the precise wording is proving a minefield. We have seen how fraught the issue of terminology can be. Almost every word in the declaration is capable of more than one interpretation. Do they talk about peoples or populations? Nations or nationalities? Independence, whether it be economic or political, sounds good, but what does it mean? Self-sufficiency sounds laudable, but what does it mean? Unfortunately, different things to different people.

Predictably, the negotiations thus far have been marred by walkouts and confusion. For example, Article 3 of the draft declaration states that:

Indigenous people have the right of self-determination. By virtue of that right they freely determine their political status and freely pursue their economic, social and cultural development.

What would this mean for the Basques? The Kurds? What about for the Maori in New Zealand?

Article 15 states that:

Indigenous children have the right to all levels and forms of education of the state. All indigenous peoples also have this right and the right to establish and control their educational systems and institutions providing education in their own languages, in a manner appropriate to their cultural methods of teaching and learning.

Indigenous children living outside their communities have the right to be provided access to education in their own culture and language.

States shall take effective measures to provide appropriate resources for these purposes.

This could have pretty far-reaching implications, depending on how it is interpreted.

Once adopted, the declaration will not be binding on member states of the UN but it will constitute a powerful moral force and will establish important political benchmarks. It is vitally important that this working group achieve its goal as the alternative is unthinkable. We must continue to seek a legal, moral and political way through, or continue to face violent threats to peace, order and progress.

But in the meantime the intentions of the draft declaration are open to wilful misinterpretation by all sorts of groups.

How do you marry collective rights (i.e. of an indigenous people) with the individual rights of citizens in a democracy based on the will of the majority? This is a worldwide issue and in New Zealand finds grave difficulties within the indigenous people themselves. The great debate in New Zealand has been between iwi (tribal) rights on the one hand and individual Maori rights on the other.

Hence the battle over the fisheries settlement. Parliament said it should benefit all Maori, but the Waitangi Fisheries Commission has defined iwi as the relevant authorities. (Indeed, they say argument for Maori non-tribal rights by a Maori is to confess to not being a Maori anyway. Not a good point at which to begin negotiations.)

This issue has been to the High Court, the Privy Council in London, and now back to the courts. Most Maori are now urban and many don't know their whakapapa. Many are learning quickly – millions of dollars are involved. But how can we claim to have reached full and final settlements when many Maori feel they have not been consulted and when their leaders are in some cases feudally appointed rather than elected in the popular sense of the word? The clash of cultures is based so often on a view of individual rights vs collective rights. New Zealand MPs at the turn of the century talked of Maori enterprise as basically communistic in nature, thus they argued it should be wiped out.

Allen Buchanan, a law professor from Wisconsin, in a paper on the theory of indigenous people's rights, points out some of the complexities:

> Collective land rights, then, are not rights which individuals, as individuals, can wield. They must be exercised, invoked, or waived non-individually, either by the group as a whole by some sort of collective decision process or by authorised agents of the collective. As rights to land, they are legal mecha-

nisms of control over land and its uses. An indefinite range of forms and degrees of control is, in principle, possible.

It is important to understand that collective land rights of both sorts not only can empower the indigenous group and limit the control which individuals and governments in the non-indigenous society have over the land and its uses; they also create authority which limits the liberty and opportunity of individuals and minorities within the indigenous group. Collective land rights confer control upon the group or its supposed representatives; in doing so, they limit the control which individuals in the group have over land.

The relationship between self-determination and collective land rights is complex, as is the fundamental principle of majority rule. Terms such as self-determination, majority rule and sovereignty are loaded with menace and danger. The danger of rising expectations and the menace of unfulfilled ambitions and the continuation of historic injustice.

In two paragraphs Buchanan puts his finger on it:

The main point is that self-determination – which means roughly, independence from domination – admits of degrees and a multiplicity of dimensions, and can take many institutional forms. The range of options, however, is limited by a simple but important fact: no group and no political unit can expect to be entirely free of all external influences. Therefore self-determination, as a realistic goal, cannot consist of complete autonomy.

Self-determination in its most extreme form is simply full sovereignty, that is, independent statehood. (Even what we call 'full' sovereignty is not complete autonomy, since even independent states are limited both by international law, including human rights, law and international trade agreements, and by every state's liability to be influenced by forces in the global economy.) Short of the extreme case of full sovereignty, there is an indefinite range of institutional arrangements whereby a group can exercise greater or lesser control over various aspects of its life. In general, a group can achieve greater or lesser self-determination depending upon how extensive the territory is within which it exercises control through collective rights and depending upon which powers it wields within that jurisdiction.

As my friend the Maori list MP Nanaia Mahuta points out, the struggle is about democratic rights versus collective rights. Free will versus the collective's will. Perhaps there will never be a common meaning; perhaps self-determination is really self-definition.

The Anglican Church in New Zealand now has a model whereby the synod, on which our Parliament is based, has a Maori and non-Maori chamber to make its laws and rules. This vision is taught at universities as an option for the future. That may be okay for an empty church. (Forgive me: I am not religious; alas, I am also an Anglican.) But for a modern nation in a global economy fuelled with the most profound and accelerating change in the history of our species?

This is not the time – there never will be a time – to jettison democracy and equality. But that's not to say that Parliament and a constitution cannot devolve authority to other structures in situations where services can be performed more effectively by those structures. We do it now in local government, in schools and in a number of other areas, so why not delegate power where it fits to iwi or other indigenous organisations?

The last time I talked to Matiu Rata before we were sadly robbed of his skill and leadership was at a New Zealand Maori Council meeting in 1997. The Maori Council was established by a National government and is the only pan-Maori structure that has been established by statute, other than the Maori seats in Parliament.

Independent of each other, we both said similar things. At a stroke, we said, if the Maori Council demanded it be directly elected, it could become the premier New Zealand-wide Maori organisation, with huge moral authority. The Alliance have this plan in their election manifesto, and good on them. Trust people – why not try democracy?

Everybody wants full and final settlements, as determined in recent legislation and as expressed in Parliament on several occasions in earlier times. But how can this be, when individual Maori frequently feel locked out of the decision-making process and don't feel the benefit of cash settlements? Maori leadership often rise to the top through feudal mechanisms. For years Maori didn't have secret ballots to elect their MPs. There was no electoral roll because it was claimed they didn't own land – an insult Australian Aborigines suffered until 1967.

The leadership of the great Maori organisations that have emerged to manage the millions of dollars in treaty settlements have not in many cases been subject to the 'indignity' of secret ballots and individual democracy, which is why their moral authority is threatened. Public companies have more democratic accountable systems than do some of the new wealthy Maori organisations.

This will end in tears, unless individuals feel part of the collective. Throughout the world indigenous people are divided into those who have power and status and those who do not. Never forget that NZ First, now in government supporting these procedures, won every Maori seat in the 1996 election on the platform of attacking what they called the Brown Table and its leadership as self-serving and greedy. Their appeal was to the disaffected Maori majority.

At last there is a general consensus among non-Maori that there has to be justice, that everyone should pay up. Their legitimate fear is that their children will have to pay up and do it again.

Democracy is an individual mandate given by the collective. That's why it is such a good management system. The mandate is only renewed with the individuals' blessing.

The traditional rights of states and individuals are enshrined in legal charters and historic treaties. But the collective rights of minorities are a much more difficult area. It incenses liberal democrats that no one ever speaks in a full and final way for indigenous peoples. But who can? Who signs the bottom line? Perhaps no one can. Because it's about values as much as it is about legal niceties and accounts.

But collective and individual rights need not be in contradiction. The collective impulse, fuelled and mandated by individual rights and elected leadership, has to be the respectful modern solution. Successful societies marry the two: look at the British House of Lords, and the mounting anger of young Maori towards their traditional leaders, who, they claim, are taking more than their share of treaty settlements and have settled for too little. But no successful society bases its power structure on inherited power. Ancestor worship is the most ancient and reactionary of all religions and cultures.

The problems do not end there. Customary rights are valid, but are not absolute – ask any endangered species. Maori women are not permitted to speak on many marae. It was not customary for women to vote in Britain until the 1920s. Female circumcision, cannibalism and slavery have all been culturally acceptable at some time. Europeans didn't invent slavery. What about the customary rights of conquest?

The controversy in New Zealand about trout fishing licences shows the problem in microcosm. The District Court said that Maori didn't need licences because trout fishing was a customary right under the Treaty of Waitangi. The High Court, on the other hand, pointed out that trout were brought to New Zealand after the signing of the treaty.

Let's get back to basics. Why do we have trout fishing licences? To maintain conservation values, to raise money to restock the rivers, and to ensure that the trout are fished at appropriate times of the year in order to sustain the species. It is intolerable if we have a situation where two citizens are fishing on the same river and one must produce a trout fishing licence and the other birth certificate. A practical solution in this instance may be a negotiated devolution of licensing for Maori to iwi (tribal) authorities, so long as conservation values are maintained.

Civilisation must march on. There cannot be a simple freeze on things. No one would want that in medical research. Technologies and ideas and principles that are dismissed as 'Western' by extremists are, in my view, in fact universal values and truths. That medical researcher may be an ethnic Indian, working in London, for an American company, financed by a Japanese company. Democratic values are universal. When the smoke clears in the killing fields, from the Congo to Cambodia, people seek their universal rights.

Indigenous peoples throughout the world are at the bottom of the barrel, scraping out a living. The descendants of slaves, African American people, can boast higher achievements than native Americans, as can more recent immigrants from the Pacific claim more rapid economic advances than many Maori. It is a danger to the cohesion of our societies and represents the stone in the shoe of our progress.

Western conceit often confuses economic modernisation with westernisation. Sure, kids in Lima, Cairo, Ruatoria and Port Moresby all wear Levis, listen to the Spice Girls, drink Coke, borrow the family Toyota and dream of a BMW. But those teenagers are torn between values and culture. Many have migrated from the countryside to the cities in pursuit of a materialistic dream. Disappointment then turns to violence and frustration and in some cases the resulting economic and social problems lead to a rejection of the materialistic ambitions. Then we experience a cultural and tribal resurgence.

That is not all bad. The dispossessed and the poor cry out that all the advances and so-called progress have left them behind. In advanced democracies the welfare state comes to the rescue, but benefits are low, and they are not the answer. 'Let my tribe/religion/cultural unit have a go!' the rural and urban dispossessed cry. 'We can't do any worse.'

This is true in varying levels of intensity in the indigenous peoples from South Auckland to Sao Paulo to Cape Town. Economic failure and unfairness provide a breeding ground for such discontent. When the poor become organised and get political the powerful tremble, and so they should. Economic security, providing faith and hope in the future, is the prerequisite to stability, progress and a better environment. Poor economics results have brought down more governments than tanks in the past decade.

So will this whole issue remain forever in the 'too hard' basket? Not while there are so many dedicated and admirable people committed to the cause of finding solutions. In a speech celebrating the 50th anniversary of the United Nations Pope John Paul II put it most eloquently:

> On the threshold of a new millennium we are witnessing an extraordinary global acceleration of that quest for freedom which is one of the great dynamics of human history. This phenomenon is not limited to any one part of the world; nor is it the expression of any single culture. Men and women throughout the world, even when threatened with violence, have taken the risk of freedom, asking to be given a place in social, political, and economic life which is commensurate with their dignity as free human beings. This universal longing for freedom is truly one of the distinguishing marks of our time.
>
> We need to clarify the essential difference between an unhealthy form of nationalism, which teaches contempt for other nations or cultures, and patriotism, which is a proper love of one's country. True patriotism never seeks to advance the well-being of one's own nation at the expense of others. For in the end this would harm one's own nation as well: doing wrong damages both aggressor and victim. Nationalism, particularly in its most radical forms, is thus the antithesis of true patriotism, and today we must ensure that extreme nationalism does not continue to give rise to new forms of the aberrations of totalitarianism. This is a commitment which also holds true, obviously, in cases where religion itself is made the basis of nationalism, as unfortunately happens in certain manifestations of so-called 'fundamentalisms'...
>
> Today the problem of nationalities forms part of a new world horizon marked by a great 'mobility' which has blurred the ethnic and cultural frontiers of the different peoples, as a result of a variety of processes such as migrations, mass media and the globalisation of the economy. And yet, precisely against this horizon of universality, we see the powerful re-emergence of a certain ethnic and cultural consciousness, as it were an explosive need for identity and survival, a sort of counterweight to the tendency towards uniformity. This is a phenomenon which must not be underestimated or regarded as a simple leftover of the past. It demands serious interpretation, and a closer examination of the levels of anthropology, ethics and law ...
>
> A presupposition of a nation's rights is certainly its right to exist: therefore no one – neither a state nor another nation, nor an international

organisation – is ever justified in asserting that an individual nation is not worthy of existence. This fundamental right to existence does not necessarily call for sovereignty as a state, since various forms of judicial aggregation between different nations are possible, as for example occurs in federal states, in confederations or in states characterised by broad regional autonomies ...

Its right to exist naturally implies that every nation also enjoys the right to its own language and culture, through which a people expresses and promotes that which I would call its fundamental spiritual sovereignty. History shows that in extreme circumstances (such as those which occurred in the land where I was born) it is precisely its culture that enables a nation to survive the loss of political and economic independence. Every nation therefore has also the right to shape its life according to its own traditions, excluding, of course, every abuse of basic human rights and in particular the oppression of minorities. Every nation has the right to build its future by providing an appropriate education for the younger generations.

Get this: There is a profound difference between cultural sovereignty and political sovereignty. That lies at the core of the argument for the rights of indigenous people and the resolution of this dilemma inside a peaceful and democratic orbit. The Vatican with its great historic insight going back over almost 2000 years offers profound truths (except where sex is concerned, for some strange reason).

The church has made significant contributions throughout history to the preservation of culture and civilised values. During the Dark Ages it was in the monasteries that literature, science and art were kept alive, ready to ignite and evolve into the age of enlightenment and the age of reason.

Indeed, at Waitangi, when New Zealand's Treaty of Waitangi was written in 1840, there was a third partner. It wasn't just the Crown and Maori: God was there too. Why did early Maori adopt so earnestly and sincerely the Christian faith? Because in the 19th century the missionaries were the good guys. They saw the injustices and savagery of unregulated European expansion. And because of their Christianity they believed we were all created equal in the image of God. We were all his children and thus all equal under his law.

That's the moral force, the moral mandate of democracy. So they sought the rule of law and a treaty to give effect to this. His representative on earth, the Crown, had a duty to uphold those laws. People believed that the Crown's authority was God-given. Kings were often upholders of the faith in more than one empire.

Thankfully we have moved beyond the liberal theory of a great melting pot. Assimilation is what the cat does to the mouse. The Marxist theory of a great global working class uniting with nothing to lose but its chains against the ruling classes was also a mirage. In his book *Future Eaters* Tim Flannery tells the story of the 'kind' missionaries and gentle and devout individuals who devoted their lived to smoothing the pillow of a dying race.

As different peoples and cultures we can face our future together or apart. Apartheid failed: it had no moral compass and could no more work than Hitler's master-race theories or Mao's cultural revolution. Perhaps we should be inspired by the new South African constitution, the preamble of which states:

> We, the people of South Africa,
> Recognise the injustices of our past;
> Honour those who suffered for justice and freedom in our land;
> Respect those who have worked to build and develop our country; and
> Believe that South Africa belongs to all who live in it, united in our diversity.
> We therefore, through our freely elected representatives, adopt this Constitution as the supreme law of the Republic so as to:
> • Heal the divisions of the past and establish a society based on democratic values, social justice and fundamental human rights;
> • Lay the foundations for a democratic and open society in which government is based on the will of the people and every citizen is equally protected by law;
> • Improve the quality of life of all citizens and free the potential of each person; and
> • Build a united and democratic South Africa able to take its rightful place as a sovereign state in the family of nations.
> May God protect our people.

New Zealand could do worse than use such language in a constitution of its own, which is why I've invested so much time in preparing legislation for a process whereby New Zealand will finally own its future through a modern constitution. Fiji progressed from a military dictatorship to a multi-racial constitution.

What's good is that nations, peoples and international institutions are addressing the issue of a painful past. What's even better, for us at least, is that New Zealand is right up there in its attempts to settle honourably and to exorcise these historic demons in a democratic spirit of reconciliation and to create rules by which peacefully to settle and arbitrate our differences.

Expect there to be a further surge in issues of cultural property and cultural rights. This is not in contradiction to globalisation; indeed, it may be the other side of the coin, which can preserve our colourful and distinct differences. We are not all the same – it would be a boring world if we were.

Modern man is impatient. We seek instant gratification. Golda Meir, the former Israeli prime minister, was abused by her opponents because the peace talks were painfully slow. She shrugged off such complaints, saying, 'At least while we are talking no boys are being killed.' Jawing is better than warring.

CHAPTER ELEVEN

Refugees: A World on the Move

THE GREATEST MOVEMENT of people in world history is under way at the moment. People are on the march in every hemisphere. There has never been anything like it in the history of our species.

Over 100 million people now live somewhere other than the land of their birth. France is home to over 3 million Islamic residents. They are legal migrants, but a new phenomenon has emerged with global implications. If all the refugees of the world, political, environmental or displaced, were added together they would constitute the seventh-largest nation on earth. Estimates vary but the United Nations High Commission for Refugees suggests there are now about 30 million traditional refugees.

The UN defines these refugees as: 'Someone who has left his or her own country or is unable to return to it owing to a well-founded fear of persecution for reasons of race, religion, nationality, membership of a particular social group or political opinion.'

The number has doubled in a decade. But there is another group of refugees today: the 90 million whom the World Watch Institute calls environmental refugees. In the last decade these people have been driven from their homes by new dams, roads, development projects and environmental degradation.

A new dam in India might force 250,000 to leave their homes, another dam in China will see a million people made homeless. Most drift towards the nearest city. The success of economic reforms in southern China has seen the greatest migration and urbanisation in that nation's long history. Up to 30 million people at any one time are on the move.

People seek economic, social, political freedom and material security and success. Urbanisation is accepted in developed societies such as the US and New Zealand but the drift to the bright lights of the cities where people see more opportunities is even more dramatic in less developed societies as large as Brazil and as small as the Cook Islands.

However, a large number of refugees are the desperate people who now receive the official and dubious status of 'internally displaced persons'.

The figures are numbing beyond rational comprehension. As Joseph Stalin said, one death is a murder, a million are a statistic. The United Nations Commission on Human Rights defines internally displaced people as 'persons or groups of persons who have been forced to flee their homes or places of habitual residence suddenly or unexpectedly as a result of armed conflict, internal strife, systematic violation of human rights or natural or man-made disasters who have not crossed an internationally recognised state border'.

The United Nations representative on Internally Displaced Persons argues that there are twice as many displaced people as traditional refugees who flee their countries of origin.

The UNHCR was established in the 1950s to handle the problems of European refugees – those who were still stateless from the world war and the new wave of people fleeing Soviet persecution and terror in Eastern Europe. Its mandate was originally for just three years. The problem is now a thousand times worse than the conditions that created this worthy office.

In an earlier century, other than the death penalty, the most feared and vicious sentence the 'powerful' handed down to the 'powerless' was internal and external exile. So what drives people to such desperate acts of flight of their own volition?

The answer is that it's that or death, fast or slow. More than 70 countries have at least 10,000 refugees inside their territories. Some 63 per cent of the population of Liberia, 45 per cent of Rwanda and Bosnia, and 20 per cent of Afghanistan, along with 3 million people in Latin America, 5 million in the Horn of Africa and 4 million in Sudan are displaced people, internal refugees.

Michael Renner in a paper called *Transforming Security* wrote:

> Traditionally, a sharp distinction has been made between migrants and refugees. Migrants are thought to leave largely of their own choosing, 'pulled' by the prospect of a better job or higher earnings, whereas refugees are compelled to vacate their homes, 'pushed' out by war, repression, or other factors beyond their control.
>
> But the categories are becoming blurred. People are increasingly leaving their homes for a mixture of reasons – both voluntary and involuntary. In some situations, migrants could be characterised as individuals who had the foresight to leave early, before local conditions deteriorated to the point where they were compelled to move – that is, before human-rights violations become massive, before economic conditions turned wretched, and before environmental deterioration made eking out an existence impossibly burdensome.

New Zealand's record on refugees is not particularly glowing. During the pre-war exodus of Jews from Nazi Germany New Zealand, along with other nations, acted shamefully. Ann Beaglehole's book *A Small Price to Pay* exposed this episode in New Zealand history, in which New Zealand officials were at pains to point out that European Jews would not be happy or fit comfortably into our homogeneous society. The few who did come to New Zealand had to pay an entry fee of £200 – a year's pay at the time.

Yet look at the commercial and social success of the very few Jews who did stay in New Zealand. They became top business people, top figures in the judiciary, great citizens. New Zealand won. Imagine if we had taken a few thousand, not a few dozen!

New Zealand later acquitted itself more honourably in bringing to New Zealand 1000 Polish orphans and lost and displaced people. After the Soviet invasion of Hungary New Zealand took more, and after the collapse of Vietnam we offered a home to over 4000 refugees. Most of those have since left to join the larger Vietnamese community in Australia.

New Zealand has taken modest numbers of refugees from Cambodia, Chile, Uganda, Iran and Somalia. In the last 50 years the US, Canada and Australia have been more generous. Germany presently plays host to over two million refugees and displaced people. The UN has a formula for the number of refugees member countries should accept to honour their international obligations. These figures are based on a percentage of the host country's total population. On this basis we have not been leaders, but we have been good average international citizens.

New Zealanders have been strangely quiet on this issue, given our propensity to lecture and even sometimes lead the world on other international issues of great moral urgency. Why has our traditional support for the underdog generally deserted us when it has come to refugees?

It's more than just a matter of the reticence of our political leadership. There needs to be a domestic constituency for brave policies and public expenditures. New Zealand's history on refugees shows that our political leaders have acted only in response to pressure from outside influences: urgings from Britain or the UN. (Refugees from Chile are one exception.) Apart from that it has been pretty much left to the churches to lobby government. It is the churches that have opened their hearts, front doors and wallets to give life to principles based on the ancient Christian concept of the right to sanctuary.

In earlier days our inaction was motivated by simple racism. Chinese orphans were not welcome; Polish orphans were. Politicians, church leaders, editors, even trade unionists spoke proudly up to the 1950s of the empire, the old country and of our proud English stock.

Latterday excuses have included issues of security. If refugees come from a Middle East country and their nation's Wellington embassiy employs more security officers to keep an eye on its former nationals how do our security services respond? Should New Zealand play host to former IRA members, former Tamil Tigers, whites fleeing from South Africa or pro-democracy leaders from China or Burma? There inevitably seem to arise complications with the governments of origin. Are these complications what an aggressive, vulnerable trading nation like New Zealand needs? Do New Zealanders really want to import such problems to our tranquil country? Aren't we proud that we don't have the racial and religious hatreds of other more ancient societies? Why import these problems? goes the official line. It's not without an appalling logic.

But that's not the formal position of the US, Germany, Canada, France, Holland or even Australia, all of which have, over the years, been more open to refugees than New Zealand. They don't use the 'security' cliché as an excuse.

What should New Zealand do? Our resources are modest, as is our influence.

In the end, the problems of refugees have to be solved at their source. They are victims of the tyranny of circumstances. That means increased support for the United Nations and its peacekeeping and peace enforcement requirements.

It means supporting trading and environmental policies internationally that allow nations to grow in a sustainable way. That means backing the World Trade Organisation in creating open trading opportunities to lift vulnerable economies. Changes under way within the IMF and World Bank to promote sustainable economic programmes need to be accelerated.

A strong domestic economy is a prerequisite for New Zealand to be able to raise and maintain domestic support for such policies. In addition, a strong New Zealand could afford to absorb at least another couple of hundred families a year. And we must ensure we don't ever again repeat the farce of the last few years where we have opened the doors to 'displaced' professionals such as doctors, only to have them hanging around, disillusioned and unemployed, because we decide too late that we don't recognise their qualifications. These people were misled. We need to accept our moral obligation to retrain and equip them to use their skills in New Zealand.

In the end no nation, small or large, can handle this enormous historical crisis on its own. That's why we have established great and noble international institutions.

Nations that create refugees are usually authoritarian. People did not flee from West to East Berlin; people are not building rafts to float from Florida to Cuba; nor are thousands of Thais escaping into Burma. History's lesson is clear. The difference between North and South Korea is like night and day. Societies that embrace change through constructive and democratic engagement produce better political and economic results.

Pro-democracy movements are thus to be cherished and supported. From Zaire to the Horn of Africa, the Balkans, Burma or Bougainville the solutions, if they are to be successful, must be mainly home grown, but cherishing and nourishing are two different things. You can pray, but you must also pay.

Ringing votes of support and well-meaning resolutions make their authors feel good. It's the politics of gestures. The hard work is diplomatic attention, both moral and financial support and encouragement for pro-democracy forces. Pay-up time is always painful. The problem is that pressure groups always want governments to go public. It can make us feel good, and that's not unimportant. But saying publicly what you believe, and saying who the good guy is, frequently disqualifies you from having any future role. If New Zealand had taken sides over Bougainville, our usefulness in that crisis would have been reduced. Like the serene swan on the lake, peacemakers need to look calm and unflustered. But under the water they are paddling like hell.

CHAPTER TWELVE

The Globalisation of the Green Movement

WHEN I WAS A CHILD we regarded the countryside as the world's biggest rubbish dump. We chopped down trees for fun, shot at anything that moved and some things that didn't, collected guns and pictures of the Second World War. We read *Moby Dick* and felt sorry for Captain Ahab. Not now. The children of today have worked out that Moby Dick is the good guy.

Everyone is for the environment. How can you be against whales and trees? It is a movement whose time has come. Political parties formed in the industrial age all now talk of the environment: this is the success of green politics. In earlier times politicians always started speeches with pious references to God and empire. Nowadays it is a nod towards sustainable development and the environment. That's good. It's progress.

If I may be allowed a note of cynicism on this most important topic, I find it unfortunate that the environment has become almost a simplistic religious mantra in some quarters, so that, for example, anything using the word 'nuclear' is bad. Well, nuclear medicine has saved thousands of cancer patients, including yours truly. Every oncology department at every hospital devotes resources to such treatments.

Alas, some today see green issues as a way of smuggling back old forms of controls. Opposition to their views apparently means you hate trees and love concrete. Business is the new Satan. Greenies have seized the high moral ground.

One of the most distasteful and condescending political techniques used by some sophisticated pressure groups to advance the green cause has been to fantasise about the so-called superior attitude of various indigenous peoples to the environment. They become token trophies. On the walls of the offices of many good people is a moving quote by the Chief Seattle of the Duwamish people:

How can you buy or sell the sky, the warmth of the land?
    The idea is strange to us.
    If we do not own the freshness of the air and the sparkle of the water, how can you buy them?

4

Every part of the Earth is sacred to my people.

Every shining pine needle, every sandy shore, every mist in the dark woods, every clear and humming insect is holy in the memory and experience of my people.

The sap which courses through the trees carries the memory and experience of my people.

The sap which courses through the trees carries the memories of the red man ...

Yadda, yadda, yadda, as Seinfeld would say.

In fact these words were actually written by Ted Perry in the 1970s for a television movie produced by the Southern Baptist Convention. Chief Seattle killed his enemies, enjoyed slaves and sold his land to the administrator of the Washington territories in 1854.

Indigenous customary rights are often in direct conflict with modern Western values of environmental protection. The right to hunt whales, kill seals, eat kereru (native pigeons) and others will test the tolerance of domestic and international law treaties. Look what happened to the North American mammoth, the South American tapir and the New Zealand moa. The Easter Islands were stripped of forests, as was Petra in Jordan. Alas, stupidity and short-sightedness is culture and colour blind. After all, it took the West thousands of years to reach the present level of green consciousness. Early Europeans were just as violent towards the environment.

Democratic societies have a better environmental record that totalitarian or authoritarian societies. Strong central control usually means no protest or green movements, and no democratic responses to problems.

Open democratic government force managers, whether in government departments or private enterprise, to be answerable and accountable to the people, inside a democratic system that has a free, inquiring and rigorous media policed by pressure groups. All are keen to keep us honest, promote their interests, and expose the corruption and inherent dishonesty of closed minds and closed systems. That's the virtue of civil society.

At a recent caucus the position that competition is bad for the environment was raised. I guess it was thought that cheaper petrol was too good for the workers. They would only misuse it. A bit like cheaper imported cars. Tell that to the rural poor who have to get their kids to school. When the proper environmental costs are internalised, i.e. manufacturers are made accountable for the environmental costs of their products, then the real costs emerge.

Then we will get a more efficient lightbulb, a more efficient hot-water cylinder, a better steel industry. Efficiency is just another word for conservation. It makes good business sense. Smart companies anticipate society's environmental ambitions and plan ahead. Many companies now market the fact that they exceed particular environmental regulations, thereby seeking to appeal to the increasingly powerful, wealthy and discerning green consumer market.

Rising incomes are the best hope for the environment. Increased affluence means people have fewer children, are better educated, and now have higher environmental expectations. That's true of every continent and atoll.

Stephen Schmidheiny, chairman of Europe's Business Council for Sustainable Development, explained to a seminar I ran at Waipuna:

> During the first great wave of environmental concern in the late 1960s and early 1970s, most of the problems seemed local: the products of individual pipes and smokestacks. The answers appeared to lie in regulating these pollution sources. When the environment re-emerged on the political agenda in the 1980s, the main concerns had become international: acid rain, depletion of the ozone layer and global warming.
>
> Analysts sought causes not in pipes and stacks but in the nature of human activities. One report after another concluded that much of what we do, many of our attempts to make 'progress', is simply unsustainable. We cannot continue in our present methods of using energy, managing urban growth, and producing industrial goods. We certainly cannot continue to reproduce our species at the present rate.
>
> The last few decades have witnessed an accelerating consumption of natural resources – consumption that is often inefficient and ill planned. Resources that are biologically renewable are not being given time to renew. The bottom line is that the human species is living more off the planet's capital and less off its interest. This is bad for business.[1]

Dunedin researcher Lloyd Godman wrote in the *Otago Daily Times* that tests showed that three-quarters of the planet's topsoil, which took millions of years to produce, had been lost in the short space of a few centuries due to inappropriate land management. *Time* magazine in June 1998 stated that 23 billion tons of topsoil is wasted or blown away every year. One Australian researcher estimated that 9kg of topsoil is lost for each loaf of bread produced.

The world's population is climbing towards 6 billion, and it is increasing by nearly 90 million a year. About 80 per cent of the world population currently lives in the developing world, and more than 80 countries – including

Nigeria, Ethiopia, El Salvador, Guatemala, Honduras and Nicaragua – are on course to double their populations over the next three decades.

Evidence is mounting that rapid population growth is the most significant cause of environmental damage, ranging from global climate change and deforestation to topsoil loss and diminishing water supply.

Overgrazing, deforestation, agricultural mismanagement and overcutting of firewood – all activities disproportionately carried out by poor people – account for 70 per cent of the damage to the world's soil, according to a United Nations study.

Werner Fornos, president of the Population Institute, points out that the destruction of tropical forests is linked to population growth, especially through migration, and results in loss of biodiversity, land degradation and emission of greenhouse gases where forests are burned, as well as depletion of a natural resource. Deforestation results from the demand for timber and from overcutting for fuelwood, with 70 per cent of the developing world's families still dependent on wood for fuel.

One thousand tonnes of water are required to produce one tonne of grain, but water tables are falling by about 20 metres per year.

Only 16 per cent of the world's farmland is irrigated. One in every 10 hectares of land is losing productivity because of salination. Most countries have not made realistic assessments of water security. The most pressing challenge, according to Fornos, is to increase the productive use of water and minimise water waste by preventing leakage and water over-usage, and recycling water where it is possible.

Much agricultural land has been lost as populations become increasingly urbanised. In 1950 less than 30 per cent of the world's population lived in the cities. Today the figure is more than 45 per cent, and it is expected to reach 60 per cent by 2025. On the Indonesian island of Java, urban and industrial growth has resulted in the loss of 20,000 hectares of agricultural land in one year, an area large enough to supply rice to 330,000 people. In China a total of 6.5 million hectares of arable land were removed from production between 1987 and 1992. Forty per cent of the loss resulted from expansion of infrastructure, industry and housing.

An international panel of scientists brought together by the United Nations as the Intergovernmental Panel on Climate Change has estimated that the world will warm by more than another half a degree over the next two decades if greenhouse emissions are not reduced. In 100 years the earth's surface is expected to be 3.5 degrees warmer than it was in 1990 – which would be the hottest in millions of years.

The likely result is widespread climatic, environmental and economic dislocation, expected to affect different regions of the world in different ways. There are likely to be more frequent and severe floods and droughts. Many low-lying coastlines and islands will disappear as sea levels rise. Entire forest types will disappear, and agriculture in some parts of the world will be devastated. Africa is likely to be the hardest hit, along with small island states in the South Pacific and Caribbean. Africa, a continent already suffering from serious water shortages and 'desertification', is particularly vulnerable because it has few resources to adapt.

At Kyoto in Japan the Kyoto Summit on Climate Change signed a protocol in late 1997 following 11 frenetic days of negotiations. The protocol requires developed countries to reduce the total emissions of greenhouse gases to 5 per cent below 1990 levels by 2012. The target for the European Union is 8 per cent below 1990 levels. The United States has a reduction target of 7 per cent, and Japan 6 per cent. Fifty-five countries – who are responsible for 55 per cent of developed countries' CO_2 emissions – must ratify the protocol for it to become international law.

Getting that far has been a major victory. New Zealand's representative at the Kyoto talks, Environment Minister Simon Upton, said that by the end of the negotiations most delegates wore expressions of 'glazed incomprehension'.

Mr Upton believes that far too many nations arrived in Kyoto with

> … the bizarre view that flexible, low-cost mechanisms were somehow bad and that prescriptive rules and regulations were the only way forward. Worse is the categorical refusal of some major players to even engage in a meaningful conversation about how in due course the world's rapidly developing economies should curb their emissions growth. Singapore once again kept a straight face in describing itself to the world as a 'developing' country, despite the fact that it is far richer than New Zealand.

The challenge for developed countries is to reduce the greenhouse effect without stalling their economies. The finger frequently points to the West as being the greater polluters. The West is concerned that without appropriate international agreement, industry and jobs will simply transfer with their pollution to the countries with less stringent environmental rules.

The *Economist* took a pragmatic approach:

You don't have to be a signed-up Green to accept that global warming is a genuine danger. But nor do you have to be Dr Pangloss to see that the danger is distant, hard to quantify, and possibly small ... These uncertainties make it difficult to decide how much insurance to buy ... Better a strong weak agreement that has a good chance of being honoured than a weak strong agreement that is likely to collapse.

Britain's *Observer* newspaper has also noted an increased reticence by many countries to submit to international direction on environmental issues. It warned that for the first time since before the Second World War

... international relations are becoming poisoned by competitive nationalisms and unwillingness even to pay lip-service to the global interest. Whether [at the] Kyoto Summit on Climate Change or in the reaction to the gathering economic crisis in Asia, we are witnessing ever-less willingness to make any concession to pressures from overseas ...

The more interdependent the world becomes, the less individual nations seem prepared to accept that their sovereignty is reduced – and that active international collaboration is a prerequisite for achieving policy goals. The madness is defined in Britain by Eurosceptics who argue the country must retain economic sovereignty even though it was lost years ago.

The *Observer* argued that what is needed is 'a new internationalism; the last bout of national rivalry led to recession and war. It's not too fanciful to imagine a repeat.'

The need to protect the biological integrity of plants and wildlife has been well understood for centuries. The Hittites prescribed a horrible death for the illicit second sowing of a field – the offender was tied between two oxen and torn apart. In the Old Testament, warring parties were urged to spare the fruit trees of their enemies, even when laying siege to their cities,

The ancient Chinese kept the secret of silkworms from the West for centuries, until, according to legend, the monopoly was broken by two Nestorian monks who bootlegged some eggs out of China in their pockets in 552 AD. One of the world's first wildlife treaties was the 1885 Convention for the Uniform Regulation of Fishing in the Rhine.

The rapid deforestation currently occurring in developing countries recalls an earlier epoch in the history of industrialised nations, when much of the world's temperate forests was cleared for agriculture, construction materials and fuelwood.

The mighty forests of the Amazon basin remained untouched for centuries until the arrival of Charles Goodyear, John Dunlop and the tyre. The best rubber in the world is said to come from the *Hevea braziliensis* tree, which grows in the Amazon and Orinoco basins.

Deforestation has attracted increasing international attention over recent years, and has resulted in a number of multilateral organisations and processes. The World Bank's forest policy now requires environmental assessments and prohibits the financing of commercial logging in moist tropical forests under any circumstances. The United Nations Conference on Environment and Development focused unprecedented attention on forest-related issues and articulated the concept of sustainable development. The Tropical Forestry Action Programme has created a framework for bringing the nations of the north and south together, and has helped many countries to analyse their forest resources more rigorously. And the International Tropical Timber Organisation has become a vehicle for conservation concerns and has established targets for sustainable tropical timber management.

The likelihood that the nations of the world will produce an international convention on forests in the foreseeable future is considered extremely slim. There is little momentum in developing countries for such an agreement. Producer countries see little need for one and fear they would be forced to pay a heavy price. Developing countries, which control 60 per cent of the world's forests, have resisted calls from industrialised countries to control their clear-cutting and logging practices.

They say it's self-serving, even immoral, for countries like New Zealand, who have destroyed more of our forest more quickly than any other nation, to take the high ground. (We can take the high ground because we have precious little forest left to save. We have wiped out 90 per cent of our birdlife and now have 10 per cent of the world's most endangered birds.) Poor countries suggest that the West pay up if it's so important. They have a point, don't they?

The Convention on Biological Diversity came into force at the end of 1993. It has been described as a long-term insurance policy for human health and welfare.

Biodiversity is critical to a country like New Zealand, which has a unique indigenous flora and an economy based on introduced plants. Dr Warren Williams, curator of the Margot Forde Forage Germplasm Centre in Palmerston North, points out that the biological diversity of other countries is of primary strategic importance to New Zealand.

Virtually the entire agricultural, horticultural and forestry industries of New Zealand, which account for a large proportion of the domestic and foreign exchange economies, are dependent on introduced plant and animal species. The maintenance and growth of this key component of the economy is dependent on continuing access to the genetic resources of other countries ... New Zealand needs to be a good global citizen and be seen to be so.

International engagement is necessary to obtain lasting results. New Zealand should support the development of international guidelines on environmental protection – out of self and global interest. But how much are we prepared to pay as our insurance premium?

Schmidheiny summed up the crux of the problem of sustainable development thus:

> It is a hard thing to demand of political leaders, especially those who rely on the votes of the living to achieve and remain in high office, that they ask those alive today to bear costs for the sake of those not yet born, and not yet voting. It is equally hard to ask anyone in business, providing goods and services to the living, to change their ways for the sake of those not yet born, and not yet acting in the marketplace. The painful truth is that the present is a relatively comfortable place for those who have reached positions of mainstream political or business leadership.
>
> ... many of those with the power to effect the necessary changes have the least motivation to alter the status quo that gave them that power.[2]

Sustainable development will require the greatest changes in the wealthiest nations, which consume the most resources, release the most pollution, and have the greatest capacity to make the necessary changes.

The difficulty, it seems, is getting people to focus on such a long-term problem. As President Clinton has said, 'We see the train coming, but most ordinary Americans in their day-to-day lives can't hear the whistle blowing.'

But, today's goal of endless economic growth in perpetuity is dishonest and fraudulent given the ecological constraints and finite resources. Environmental policy and conservation goals are essentials in long-term efficiency planning. The market will work if the correct signals are sent and people pay the true price of pollution. Faced with paying the true cost of power, just imagine what energy and conservation products business would develop!

We need new systems of accounting. Our measurement of wealth, growth and gross national product (GNP) is based on out-of-date accounting practices that were written in an age when resources were seen as infinite. They were the days of the pioneers and the wild west, when nature was to be conquered.

Al Gore's book *Earth In the Balance* has a powerful and profound chapter on economics. He argues that in calculating GNP, natural resources should be depreciated in economic terms as they are used up.

Buildings and factories are depreciated, so why hasn't the topsoil in Iowa depreciated when it wastes down the Mississippi after certain agricultural methods have lessened its ability to resist wind and rain? Because we fail to see value in growing grain in an ecologically sound manner, we have lost half the topsoil of Iowa. The heavy use of pesticides may ensure that the grain we grow achieves the highest possible short-term profits, but the careless and excessive use of pesticides contaminates the groundwater reservoirs beneath the field. When we add up the costs and benefits of growing grain, the loss of the fresh water resource will he ignored. Because we fail to measure the true cost of clean, fresh underground water, we have contaminated more than half of all the underground reservoirs in the United States.

In the international sphere, Gore writes:

When an under-developed nation cuts down a million acres of tropical rainforest in a year, the money earned is counted as that nation's income for the year. The wear and tear on the chainsaws and trucks will be entered on the expense side of the ledger, but the wear and tear on the forest will not.

This is absurd yet, as Gore points out, the World Bank, the IMF, development banks and credit agencies have contributed to this problem by measuring the growth and wealth of nations in a system that rewards the ravaging of the environment. The despoilers are the most 'creditworthy', so the more pollution, the greater the GNP and productivity!

The *Exxon Valdez* oil spill and the efforts to clean it up actually increased the GDP of the US. If we cut down every tree in New Zealand in one year, under current accounting practices it would be a boom year. Thankfully there has been some progress within the World Bank on this issue since Gore wrote his book.

Recently the European Roundtable representing big business interests pledged itself to environmental change:

The introduction of sustainable development will have a revolutionary effect as far reaching as the introduction of steam, electricity and electronics in their time. It is, above all, an intellectual revolution.[3]

Environmental protection is a growth industry. Environmental protection and management enterprises are among the fastest growing and most profitable in the world. In Canada there are 200,000 jobs already in this industry, generating around $825 billion worth of economic activity in 1992 and growing at 12 per cent a year. What is tourism other than environmental voyeurism? There need not be a contradiction. Saving the environment is good business.

This spin-off is that higher individual national standards lead to higher international standards. In 1987 the 10 largest market economies spent more than $240 billion on pollution control.

California has some of the toughest environmental rules in the world and its environmental services industry is worth $260 billion. The potential is infinite. The United States has decided to spend $400 billion over the next decade to clean up its military and energy facilities. Taiwan, which has now surpassed many developed nations, is looking to spend $80 billion to clean up its environment.

I was in China several years ago and met a great New Zealander, Rewi Alley. One of our delegation asked Alley what he most wanted to do for the Chinese people before he died. Alley laughed and replied:

'I want to do two things. I want to get the Chinese into shorts, and I want to encourage them to reafforest the mountains.' He was concerned about massive loss of life due to flooding. Cutting down the forests has increased erosion, so that rivers are becoming clogged and prone to flooding.

Many of the great and ancient cultures of the world – Turkey, India, China and north Africa – have progressively destroyed their ancient forests. And many today are addressing the problem of what to do about it. It took them thousands of years – we Kiwis did it in less than 100 years.

What a splendid opportunity for New Zealand. Think of the jobs and costs involved in saving and rebuilding these forests. New Zealand has the technology to assist. In the 1980s a Labour government helped set up an enterprise at Lincoln University called Lincoln International, to market the skills and expertise at that institution throughout the world. (We once gave free lectures to our competitors on how to grow kiwifruit. I stopped that nonsense.)

We can plant forests from aircraft, packing fertiliser with the seeds before airdropping them.

Tough laws to clean up our rivers forced our wool scourers to upgrade their technology, to either become more efficient or perish. Annett and Darling in Timaru sell some of the best wool-scouring technology all around the world, from Korea to Eastern Europe to South America. We were able to assist them in a modest way by ensuring that some of our aid money went to help build a plant in Eastern Europe, providing clean water and producing lanolin.

In the past we have exported our pollution by sending our greasy wool away so that it was cleaned in someone else's river. Now we must export our clean wool and clean technologies. In an interconnected world with future international regimes on pollution, the opportunities for an enterprising nation are endless.

Our whole tourism industry is prefaced on our 'clean and green' environment. We take it for granted, but a Swiss hitchhiker once told me he came to live in New Zealand because he was so impressed that we dried our washing on outside clotheslines! It might seem a small thing, but through much of the world the pollution is so bad that a white shirt turns grey within half an hour. We also take for granted our ability to turn on a tap and drink a glass of fresh, clean water. How many nations on earth can do that?

We stopped spearing and netting cattle generations ago as the hunter-gatherer tribal society gave way to the agricultural economy. Yet we still hook and net fish.

We have yet to seriously begin fish farming. Yet one billion people, a fifth of the world's population, enjoy fish as their major source of protein. Sustainable aquaculture has to be one of the great industries of the future.

One day we will harvest seaweed and kelp as we do maize, and we will graze fish as we do sheep. Then those who have a commercial advantage will be the most zealous green guardians of the environment.

New Zealand was a pioneer in managing fishing grounds by offering ownership and tenure by a quota system. Eventually we will treat the sea as we do land. Areas will be set aside for different uses: residential, commercial, recreational or environmentally pristine as a national park, just as we now do for land.

So successful have our management systems been for fisheries, even the structure of our national parks and postal services, that these skills have become an income-earner as we now sell these ideas and experience overseas. Delegations arrive in New Zealand to study our advances and take the system back home. Our forest management skills of sustainable logging, and the way we allocate fisheries, are of international interest.

New Zealand Post now earns over $10 million a year selling management systems that will improve efficiencies in other countries. New Zealand customs officers fan out to places like Sri Lanka, Conservation Department staff brief Hungarians on how to establish national parks, Treasury officials talk to Thais about open budget processes, Foreign Affairs organises seminars for

Indonesian colonels on international law and human rights. We take much for granted in New Zealand. These experiences, born out of our economic restructuring, were painfully learnt.

We also take for granted our farming ability. In Hungary and much of Eastern Europe they have to bring the sheep inside during the coldest winter months. The costs of heating are enormous and the pollution problems of the waste immense, as is danger of disease. In New Zealand we developed breeds of sheep that can live on the sides of mountains in winter. The technology of breeding sheep for the right climate is now for sale internationally. New Zealand built a model farm in Hungary which has become a showcase, a permanent trade fair selling our electric fences, our seed and oil wool presses, our skills and our technology.

So-called 'eco-industries' have to be encouraged by vision, by venture capital, by a partnership and marriage of government and business. The great re search and educational institutions of technology and progress are not the enemy of the environment, but its saviour. Think of the paper saved with an electronic post office! Market forces, controlled and encouraged, can work. Children now queue at petrol stations recycling aluminium cans into machines that give them prizes on a random basis.

Alvin Toffler wrote in *Creating a New Civilization* that what makes the information age different is that

> … while land, labor, raw materials and perhaps even capital can be regarded as finite resources, knowledge is for all intents inexhaustible. Unlike a single blast furnace or assembly line, knowledge can be used by two companies at the same time. And they can use it to generate still more knowledge.

It's happening now. Science and technology are not a threat to the environment, indeed, efficiencies in the marketplace are the best policy to save the environment. The US uses less steel today than it did in 1960, while its GNP has gone up 250 per cent. Why? Proper environmental costing forced investment into alterations and better efficiencies – something that never happened in the old Marxist world.

Japan has the best steel industry in the world, but it has neither iron or coal. Perhaps that's why. Japan is a smart importer as well as a smart exporter. The Japanese are not locked into low-quality, bad-supply coal, as were the British or the Americans. They can buy it wherever the price is the most competitive. Not having resources is not a barrier to becoming rich – it's often the opposite.

'The strongest proof that environmental protection does not hamper competitiveness,' says Harvard Business School professor Michael Porter, 'is the economic performance of nations with the strictest laws.' He points to the successes of Japan, Germany and the US in sectors subject to the greatest environmental costs such as chemicals, plastics and paints.

A compelling commercial case can be made for the preservation of unspoiled environments as nations' potential treasure troves. Researchers say the rainforests may hold the key to the treatment of cancer, Aids and other diseases. Over 1.5 million plant species have been registered, although there may be 100 million different species, of which 8 per cent are to be found in rainforests.

There is a commercial rush to find new products from the forests. Some 25 per cent of all prescription drugs are derived from plants: the biotech industry is worth $2 billion per annum and is predicted to soar to $50 billion within the decade. Cancer-fighting products from plants as diverse as broccoli and the yew tree have excited pharmaceutical boardrooms.

Science and its life-saving potential are the best allies of the forests and thus indigenous peoples' habitat in many parts of the world. Dr Michael Balick, director of the Institute of Environmental Economics in New York, has found that herbal products could return $1346 per acre on a sustainable yield, compared with $137 per acre in Brazil and $117 per acre in Guatemala.

Donations of aid and international assistance packages are laudable, but pale in comparison with the financial muscle of the transnational corporations. Says Dr Balick:

> It seems clear now the decision whether to cut down a forest or preserve it revolves around the question of how much money a farmer can make, how effectively he or she can feed the family. One of our jobs is to find an economically viable alternative to deforestation.

Nations now realise there must be international solidarity to ensure results in this area. Commerce, given the correct economic signals, has the ability to adapt and create new products and innovations to achieve more sustainable results. When governments try to control and subsidise outcomes, they make things worse and stall progress.

Reality is the mother of invention and the parent of change. The children at school today can be trusted to do better than my 'greedy generation'. It's we who have consumed more of the world's resources than nearly all the other generations put together since our species began to walk upright.

Given local democracy and a progressive internationalist approach, the profound interest, idealism and commitment of the young will see the next generation do better.

When I was a kid, our classroom and bedroom walls had pictures of guns and fighter planes on them. Today's classrooms are covered in pictures of whales and penguins. I get great enjoyment out of visiting schools throughout New Zealand. I am invited to speak but it is from listening to the young people that I draw my inspiration. The children enthusiastically discuss their project – from cleaning up the beaches to organising recycling drives.

It is the young people who now lead the adults. The young scold their parents about smoking, tell them not to drink and pick up their rubbish behind them. It is the children, shopping with their parents, who tell the adults to buy milk in cardboard rather than plastic containers.

The young at school today will be the first generation since 1945 who will not live in the foreboding shadow of a nuclear holocaust. They will not be driven by the imperatives of the Cold War. For them, the issue of the day is the kind of world they will inherit. Our world was in danger of destroying itself in a nuclear wipe-out. They live in fear of an environmental wipe-out.

Mine was the lucky generation. Too young for the war, missed the Great Depression, enjoyed free milk in school, the wool boom, free education, the defining change in the relationship between the sexes, the liberation of the pill. Today's youngsters face the fear of Aids. Ours was a generation of hope and possibilities. Every political statement began: 'If we can land a man in the moon we can cure cancer, if we can do this and that then we can solve unemployment …'

Our political heroes were optimists, idealists, happy warriors who spoke to the finest attributes of our species. J.F.K., Martin Luther King, Norman Kirk remain immortal because they were cruelly taken from us so early and abruptly.

Hope and expectations were high in the 1960s and 70s. Anything seemed possible. In the 1980s and 90s sophisticated political consultants poll and research what voters think or worry about and then target messages to those disaffected. This is the antithesis of leadership. Lower tax, more expenditure and glib 8.5-second TV grabs are no substitute for leadership. There is a law, a political formula, that works like this: Promise, minus result, equals cynicism and disillusionment, which in turn equals falling trust, faith and confidence in our institutions, laws and civil society.

As Pope John said, a cohesive society is based on faith, justice, hope and trust. But can you blame the young for not having any of those emotional principles? It's not their fault, is it? Who stripped them of their faith, hope and trust?

CHAPTER THIRTEEN

Hope for the Millennium

*Integrity without knowledge is weak and useless, and knowledge
without integrity is dangerous and dreadful.* – Samuel Johnson, 1759

THE MILLENNIUM WILL attract the inevitable industry of Doomsday books, and people who make a living out of scaring themselves and others. Therefore it is appropriate to study some of the predictions of these people over the ages and enjoy their embarrassment.

Consider the state of the world a little more than a decade ago. All of South America, much of Asia, all of Eastern and central Europe and Africa, were governed by parties of either the extreme right or the extreme left. None of these countries enjoyed much economic, political, social or environmental freedom.

Now name a time in world history when so many people and so many nations could enjoy more freedom of the polling place and the marketplace than they can today. I believe these two freedoms are linked. The democratic, political and economic ideal is on the march. What's the first thing an oppressed person calls for once liberated, from the Congo to Cambodia, from Poland to South Africa? The chance, the freedom to vote! These are not just European values, they are universal values.

The Berlin Wall has come down. The Iron Curtain has been shredded, and those people enslaved since the Second World War set free. Who would have dreamed that Nelson Mandela would lead his country to peaceful freedom? Who would have thought that in government, the African National Congress would be able to enlist the support of the minority whites? The great exodus of white capital and people that was predicted has not eventuated.

Throughout South America many right-wing military governments have all but evaporated: in Argentina, Chile, Peru, Brazil, even Paraguay. Freedoms have been advanced in every one of those countries. Postwar Vietnam is set to become a new Asian tiger. The Hong Kong changeover was peaceful! Who would have believed 10 years ago that even in the Middle East there is a glimmer of hope, a chance for peace, and a Palestinian territory established and evolving? In Northern Ireland there are better hopes for peace than for 100 years. Who would have believed that NATO would be expanding to take into its fold nations that once were enemies?

Of course peace isn't perfect. Progress is never in a straight line, but the overwhelming march of history has been a positive one, especially over past 50 years.

As a teenager I was employed in the printing industry as a stationery storeman. More stationary than stationery, actually, allowing me to sell raffle tickets and work for the Labour movement. Later, I worked for the best boss I ever had, Barry Underwood in Otahuhu, who ran a small printing business behind his house. In those days there were six separate and specialist trades involved in newspaper production: journalist, subeditor, typesetter, compositor, platemaker and printer.

Now the journalist and subeditor can type straight into the computer, which spellchecks and produces the plates for the printer. Technology is now available that converts the spoken word to text. No typists? One hundred years ago a worker had to work for a day to purchase a copy of *The Times*; now it takes only a few minutes of work to pay for a copy. Free newspapers clog the letterbox and compete with free-to-air TV and radio. Talkbacks are letters to the editor without an editor to sieve them.

Only 130 years ago a worker in England had to work a full week to pay for *one word* in an international telegram to New Zealand. Now someone on the unemployment benefit needs to receive only an hour's benefit to pay for a full fax to be sent to England.

In my childhood it was the dream of every ambitious working-class parent to give his or her children a set of the *Encyclopaedia Britannica*. Back then that took almost a year's pay, but nowadays it's available on CD and costs a week's work, with updates available even more cheaply. Bowling clubs can produce sophisticated newsletters with cartoons and graphics. When I first came to Parliament we were running hand-driven, messy duplicators.

I was one who thought that the new age of information and technology would enslave people. George Orwell's *1984* convinced me that information and technology would be used by great corporations and powerful governments to suppress individuals and disturb their march to freedom.

In fact, the opposite has happened. One of the reasons that Eastern Europe is free is that governments could no longer control information. Ask the cop who beat up Rodney King in Los Angeles. No one in authority knows who might have a hand-held video camera. Television cameras make everyone witnesses to events that make history. Remember watching the Gulf War on CNN? Foreign ministers can see at the same time as the public what's happening in Iraq, or watch a press conference of the president of the USA.

We all have carved in our collective memories the TV shots of the Berlin Wall coming down, Nelson Mandela's smile and dance of freedom, and the sight of the brave young man standing in front of a tank in Tienanmen Square. Tyrants beware: we can all see you now. (Of course this doesn't stop the nutters in North Korea producing TVs with only one channel.) Bibles could not be banned forever in the Soviet Union. The airwaves, faxes and cellphones tell the story, and blow the cover of the powerful.

The political spin-doctors and the authoritarian dictators try to stay on top, but with the explosion of information, their powers are in decline. I can sit at my house in Christchurch and watch two local TV channels, two central news programmes, and the BBC and CNN. Auckland now has more radio stations than Sydney.

There are still human-rights abuses, there is still pain and poverty. We have a long way to go – but look how far we have come. If you take in the big picture, the direction of change is unmistakable.

American resource economist Julian Simon wrote a very important book entitled *The State of Humanity* in which he convincingly described the amazing story of the advancement of the human species:

> Almost every absolute change and the absolute component of almost every economic and social change or trend points in a positive direction, so long as we view the matter over a reasonably long period of time.

Only 10,000 years ago our ancestors were hunters. Around this time they first discovered agriculture and built permanent homes. This, the first agricultural revolution, increased food supply and these urban developments created an opportunity for a peaceful civilisation.

Yes, there was a dark age in Europe but there was also an age of enlightenment, of reason and renaissance. In the age of Mozart many people were so malnourished they could not work more than a few hours a day. Two hundred years and an industrial revolution later the difference in living standards is phenomenal. According to one estimate, in 16 developed countries per capita income was 13 times higher in 1979 than in 1820. Almost all populations of Western countries have shared in this transformation of material conditions.

Professional cynics will say it's uneven. Of course it's uneven. That's no reason to stop. It's even less an excuse to go backwards to a more uneven time. There is an argument that the rich are getting richer and the poor are getting poorer, but even that's not universally true. African Americans' incomes are 26 times higher than they were in the late 1860s. In the United States over 60 per cent of all households officially classified as poor have one or more cars, and half have air conditioning. An average family of four technically defined as poor in the US has twice the income of the average worker at the turn of the century.

When I was a child only the wealthy had television. Now people on the most modest incomes own freezers, televisions and videos. For thousands of years life expectancy was around 20-30 years. By the 17th century it was 30-40 years. Life expectancy in the developed world now stands at 70-80 years. We have doubled the average lifespan since the century of Milton and Newton.

Third World trends are even more dramatic. At the turn of the century life expectancy in the developing world was below 30 years: now it's over 60. In real terms, absolute poverty has been halved for most developed countries in the last 20 years. Clean water, better food and housing and basic drugs have played an important role in raising life expectancy.

There has also been a dramatic fall in the rate of child mortality. In pre-industrial Europe between a quarter and a half of all children died before the age of five. Obviously the Third World still lags substantially behind most developed countries in this statistic, but child mortality rates have been declining in all continents.

Until the last half of this century most doctors did more harm than good for patients. The agonies of unassisted childbirth, or of operations without anaesthetic, are things of the past.

Working hours have declined from around 60 hours a week in the middle of last century to under 40 hours today. People are taking much longer holidays and different kinds of holidays. Last century only the aristocrats and the wealthy – and the occasional New Zealand politician – could afford the Grand Tour of Europe. Now most New Zealand kids travel overseas. The term OE is part of our vocabulary.

Twenty years ago a pensioner could not afford a car. Now because of progressive policies of opening our economy to imports, many pensioners have Honda cars made in the 1980s. This can't be bad.

Look at education. Last century very few people got educated. Today school enrolment in New Zealand is compulsory. Illiteracy in this country has been virtually abolished. Adult illiteracy in the Third World has fallen spectacularly.

Last century it was predicted by economist Stanley Jevons that Britain would be destroyed as a superpower because it would run out of coal. It was also reported to London authorities that London would be buried in horse manure, such was the growth of hansom cabs. Remember the Club of Rome suggesting there would be a great depression – if not the end of the world – because of resource scarcity? They predicted in *The Limits to Growth* in 1972 that gold would be exhausted by 1981, tin by 1987, petroleum by 1992, and copper, lead and natural gas by 1993.

It's in the area of food production that the most scare tactics have been employed. I was one of a generation that was always reminded by Mum that you ought to eat all your food because of the starving people in China and India. We collected Corso gifts for people in Singapore; they now have a higher dollar income than us, a lower infant mortality rate and longer life expectancy.

Today very few people are starving in China and India. There has been a spectacular success via the green revolution, which has doubled the output of food over the last 30 years. There has been little significant expansion in land area used for agriculture. Productivity improvements have brought about a huge reduction in the percentage of the labour force involved in agriculture, from well over 50 per cent in most Western countries prior to the industrial revolution to under 5 per cent today. The long-run trend of food prices relative to income is down.

Paul Erlich, whose bestsellers predicted 20 years ago that the world was teetering on the brink of mass starvation, has been proven wrong. School children were told the planet would be uninhabitable by the year 2000. In only one region has the food situation deteriorated and that is Africa. There, drought frequently causes famines, which were exacerbated by Marxist and military governments, civil war and regional conflict.

But most Marxists have been discredited and beaten, even in Africa.

Collectivisation failed; Mao Zedong's great leap forward was a leap backwards that cost 30 million lives and lost China a generation. Now that private farmers have been allowed to get on with the job and to own their own products, food production in China has flourished. They are now food exporters as well as importers.

Last century pollution was far worse than it is today. In the 17th century Londoners were breathing what diarist John Evelyn called 'impure and thick mist accompanied by filthy vapour corrupting the lungs'. In the 19th century London fog was still notorious. Now, for the first time in several generations, fish are being caught in the Thames. Charles Dickens would not recognise London today. The smog has been virtually eliminated.

Some of the American/Canadian Great Lakes were considered dead 25 years ago and some rivers often caught fire. Today 70 per cent of the area's rivers are considered safe for swimming or fishing, compared with 36 per cent in 1972. Ocean dumping of industrial waste has been reduced by 94 per cent. The total forested areas in the world's temperate regions actually increased between 1980 and 1990.

Of course there is much to be done, but my central message is more than one of hope, it is one of practical success. The extreme greens and those who are always predicting the end of the world often suggest there needs to be more state control to prevent environmental disasters. But in fact the most appalling cases have occurred in economies that have been tightly controlled and tightly regulated. Look at Eastern Europe. The Volga and the Don are open sewers. In Central Asia the greatest man-made catastrophe ever is the Aral Sea. Three-quarters of the old Soviet Union's water system surface water is polluted. In the Soviet Union life expectancy had dropped over the last 30 years, which is counter to the trend through most of Europe.

Remember the Rev Thomas Malthus, who predicted that rising populations in Britain and throughout the world would lead to mass famines? And *Silent Spring* by Rachel Carson, in which she predicted in 1962 that man-made chemicals would wipe us all out within 20 years?

In 1970 Stephen Schneider predicted a new ice age, as did the respected journal *Science Digest*. Yet within a few years we have moved into something more like a global sauna. In 1980 acid rain was going to kill all the forests in Europe and North America. In 1984 the UN environmental programme claimed that a quarter of the world's surface would become deserts. There has been no net increase in global desert area over the last 10 years.

In 1991 Carl Sagan suggested that smoke from the torched Kuwaiti oil wells would lower global temperature, and cause drought and famine in India and massive agricultural failure in the United States.

There is no end to those who are prepared to make money and fame out of predicting failure and underestimating the intelligence of the people.

The argument that the rich are consuming too much of the world's resources and will eventually overpopulate the world is also off target. The opposite is the truth. We need more rich and educated people.

As countries get richer people become better educated. The size of families declines, the population drops. They demand better and more democratic political, economic, social and environmental outcomes. When given a chance to choose, people choose liberty and progress.

I'm going to be even more controversial and politically incorrect. The reality is that market economies look after the environment better, and that democracy and the ingenuity of our species know no bounds when freedom unleashes the genius of the people. Look at the way in which we, in New Zealand, have managed to organise sustainable fishing and forestry over the last decade. A world first.

The successful quota scheme for fisheries is a textbook example of the environmental benefits of securing property rights. In the 1980s the Labour government promoted New Zealand's natural environment by allowing the market to work and taking the state out of business.

We cut out the swamp drainage subsidies; abolished the land development and encouragement loan schemes that had funded the clearance of 30,000 hectares of native forests since 1978; stopped concessional finance for building local authority hydro-electric dams; abolished tax concessions for land clearance by forestry companies; got rid of special tax deals for mining companies; corporatised state enterprises; and stopped the building of state-owned Think Big projects.

The key factor in building this better world has been the growth of universal democratic values. Democratic political and economic values lift living standards. Where people have higher living standards and a better education they expect more from their environment and from their society. Where there is no democracy, no civil society, no green movement, no protesters, no free media and no Parliament, Marxist and fascist economies can pollute to their hearts' content.

I don't underestimate the social dislocation and the lack of social cohesion in New Zealand, the amount of domestic violence or the amount of unemployment. Nor do I believe the costs of the last 20 years have fallen fairly, but I do believe things are better than they were and will get better.

Take issues of gender and racial differences. When I was at school children were punished for speaking Maori. Now Maori is taught in most schools. We are advancing on Treaty of Waitangi issues. Indigenous rights are on the world's agenda.

Britain did not become a true democracy until the 1920s when women got the vote but in New Zealand women have been exercising their democratic right since 1893. Sexist and racist jokes are no longer funny. In fact 'political correctness' is now so much in vogue it has come to represent a humourless, boring, cowardly conformity.

One of the most fundamental changes in our social system in my lifetime has been in regard to matrimonial property. When I was first an MP if a woman left her husband and had not been in the paid workforce, she got nothing. Not a bean. I used to meet with women who had only the clothes they stood up in. That has changed. We provide houses and benefits – never enough houses, never large enough benefits – but this must be an advance.

It's unfashionable to be positive, optimistic and full of hope. But I am and I believe that if you researched every social indicator, from literacy to health to pollution, to compare levels between 1900 and the year 2000, you would find that the world has got better in every sphere.

We've built up great international institutions that serve the world. With all their imperfections, a world without them would be unthinkable. We have international laws on the sea. We're building up a regime of international laws on pollution. We're stopping the slaughter of whales. We have regimes in place to protect endangered species. There's a way to go in all of these areas but we ought not to wander around oppressed and apologetic or ashamed.

The year 2000 will create a new industry of black arm-band wearers and whingers. The flat-earth and end-of-the-world types will take a high profile. But we should stand with pride because we are on the threshold of delivering longer and more sustained peace, longer and more sustained economic growth and a fairer and better society. Some 1.5 billion people have had their living standards doubled over the past 15 years.

What kind of century will the next one be? Some may argue that it will be a decade of new higher moral standards, others say it will be the exact opposite, with a further breakdown of the existing social fabric. Obviously the shapes of families will continue to change. In agricultural and feudal societies three generations lived in one home. With the industrial society came the nuclear family with education of children, and health care of the elderly frequently contracted out. This freed up parents to work in the mills, mines and shops.

Soon the nuclear family will be in a minority. People live longer, women have more options, thanks to contraception and the welfare state. People are no longer trapped by oppressive religious laws or conventions and can make new choices.

Can we predict the direction of change? No, only that it will accelerate. Japanese forecasters say 80 per cent of the new jobs next century will be based on products we have yet to invent. That's a test of conservative bankers and investors! Would you risk your savings on this promise?

Prophecy is a risky business. We only have to flip through the forecasts of the past decades to find more prophets who were proved wrong.

In 1980 experts were sure that compact discs containing millions of words would make books obsolete. Yet books still abound and CD reference libraries are hardly to be seen.

In 1960 the experts said that future movies would be seen in 3D, but 3D turned into a flop.

When typewriters came into being, it was predicted that people would soon lose the ability to write manually.

It was predicted that television would be the death of radio. Radio today is stronger than ever.

Our great-grandparents would be astounded. In their world there were no aeroplanes, cars, computers or telecommunications. No one had ever heard a radio or seen a television show. Add to this refrigeration, power, climate control, space travel, automatic washing machines, dishwashers, microwaves, instant hot water and the list goes on.

Marie Curie had brilliant intuitions about radium, but no one else, including her, could have foreseen the Hiroshima bomb, or the politics of a nuclear age. Even up to 1960 infections such as diphtheria and whooping cough were still fearsome killers. No one could have imagined today's antibiotics. Now the new-immune free diseases and their rapid spread through the world poses one of the real threats of the century.

In less than half a century since they began to be widely used, computers have solved most of the old problems of computation and process control. Computers have invaded and enhanced our lives. In fact it is hard to think of any area in which computers have not had an impact.

Prices of technology relative to income have plummeted. When I was born in 1949 a six-valve radio cost more than a brand-new three-piece lounge suite.

Long ago, through controlled breeding, humans began to produce new varieties of dogs. Pekinese, Great Danes, Pit Bull Terriers, Golden Retrievers, the Mexican Hairless and the Old English Sheepdog are the result of human intervention in the canine gene pool.

We have improved on sheep, cattle and deer breeds. That's also true of crops since the beginning of the agricultural age. It's only the speed and pace of change that have changed. The use of DNA technology will surely continue. It may be possible to produce in animals a natural and inheritable immunity to certain disease by utilising DNA technology.

Genetic engineering of the human race is in today's terms frightening. Even with bans on uncontrolled eugenics a black market in recombinant DNA technology is sure to emerge. Supersports teams at the Olympics? Will science save the Warriors league team?

Science without morality, technology without honour, business without humanity, logic without faith and government without compassion end up as some sort of totalitarianism. Never forget than tribes can be led astray by psychopaths who burn books, kill sparrows and abuse their teachers in cultural revolutions. Hitler got his theories of eugenics from Engels and Marx's *The Nationalities Question*. This was later put into deadly effectiveness by Lenin, who talked of 'inferior, incurable or reactionary tribes and classes'. H.G. Wells, still a respected figure among democratic socialists, spoke similarly.

We cannot expect perfection. So what? Be encouraged: the Paris City Council once opposed the building of the Eiffel Tower. Anyhow, perfection means an end. There is no end. And remember, you can never trust leaders without a sense of humour. Fanatics have no insight, no sense of humour, and their kings have no clothes.

The truth is that no one knows the future. We can only prepare for it, be flexible and adaptable. Harry Warner thought 'talkies' would never replace the silent movies. The richest man in the world, Bill Gates of Microsoft, was originally dismissive of the Internet.

As Matt Ridley sadly concluded in *The Origins of Virtue*:

> The Hobbesian search for a perfect society ended therefore in the gas chambers of Auschwitz, expressing not the human instinct for co-operation but the human instinct for genocidal tribalism, the Faustian bargain that comes, as we have seen, with groupishness.

Globalisation and the new democratic internationalism that must accompany it provide our best hope for growth and stability. Interdependence and co-operation are replacing confrontation in many areas of human endeavour, creating a safer, more prosperous world. A world ruled by law and democratic instincts and institutions is a splendid ambition. It will not be seamless or perfect. Peace and progress are always fragile – after all, they are man-made – but let's celebrate because it is a time of hope. It is not a time of faith and trust. Hope springs eternal; trust and faith must be learned. That's the greatest challenge for today's leaders.

CHAPTER NOTES

Acknowledgments and Preface
1. Renato Ruggiero, WTO Director General, in a speech in 1998.

Chapter 1
1. Horner and Owens, writing for the International Bureau of Fiscal Documentation Office, OECD.
2. US Commerce Department statistics, May 1998.
3. *Time*, December 1997.
4. Ibid.
5. Horner and Owens, op. cit.
6. Alan Greenspan, speech in Miami, Florida, 1998.
7. John Naisbitt, *Megatrends: Transforming Our Lives*, Warner Books, 1984.
8. John Naisbitt and Patricia Aburdene, *Megatrends 2000: Ten New Directions for the 1990's*, Morrow, 1990.

Chapter 3
1. Adam Smith, *An Inquiry into the Nature and Causes of the Wealth of Nations*, 1776 (reprinted Methuen, 1950).
2. Adam Smith, *The Theory of Moral Sentiments* or *An Essay: A Dissertation on the Origin of Languages*, Wells and Lilly, 1817 (reprinted Regnery Pub., 1997).
3. Charles Darwin, *On the Origin of Species*, 1859 (reprinted Prometheus Books, 1991).

Chapter 4
1. Richard John Seddon, NZ Prime Minister 1893-1906; Michael Joseph Savage, NZ Prime Minister 1935-40.
2. GAO, 'North American Free Trade Agreement: Impacts and Implementation', statement before the US Subcommittee on Trade of the House Committee on Ways and Means, 11 September 1997. I am indebted to an article by Daniel Griswold, 'The Fast Track to Freer Trade', Cato Institute, 30 October 1997, which drew attention to this US government study.
3. *Journal of Commerce*, 13 November 1997.
4. 'Europe's Structural and Competitiveness Problems and the Euro', by Dominick Salvatore, *Journal of World Trade*, 1998.
5. Renato Ruggiero, WTO Director General, in a speech to celebrate the 50th anniversary of GATT, 4 March 1998.

Chapter 5
1. Jessica T. Mathews writing in *Foreign Affairs*, 1998.

Chapter 10
1. Malcolm N. Shaw, *International Law*, Cambridge University Press, 1997.
2. Boutros Boutros-Ghali, *An Agenda for Peace*, United Nations, 1992.

Chapter 12

1. Stephen Schmidheiny in *New Zealand, A Nation That Can Work Again, The Proceedings of the Waipuna Seminar*, MMSC Ltd, 1993.
2. Ibid.
3. Ibid.

BIBLIOGRAPHY AND FURTHER READING

Archie, Carol, *Maori Sovereignty: The Pakeha Perspective*, Hodder Moa Beckett, 1995.

Beaglehole, Ann, *A Small Price to Pay*, Allen & Unwin: Historical Branch, 1988.

Belich, James, *Making Peoples*, Penguin, 1996.

Bellamy, Christopher, *Knights in White Armour*, Hutchinson, 1996.

Bevan, Aneurin, *In Place of Fear*, MacGibbon and Kee, 1961.

Buck, Peter, *Vikings of the Sunrise*, 1938.

Cochrane, Peter, *Tips for Time Travellers*, Orion Business Books, 1997.

Crocombe, Graham T., Enright, Michael J., Porter, Michael E., with Caughey, Tony, *Upgrading New Zealand's Competitive Advantage*, New Zealand Government, 1991.

Crocombe, Ron, *Pacific Neighbours*, Centre for Pacific Studies, University of Canterbury, 1992.

Daly, Herman E. & Cobb, John B. Jr, *For the Common Good*, Beacon Press, 1989.

Davidson, James D. & Rees-Mogg, Lord William, *The Sovereign Individual*, Simon & Schuster, 1997.

Darwin, Charles, *On the Origin of Species*, 1859 (reprinted Prometheus Books, 1991).

Diamond, Jared M., *Guns, Germs, and Steel*, Norton, 1997.

Disraeli, Benjamin, *Sybil* or *The Two Nations*, reprinted London Folio Society, 1983.

Drucker, Peter F., *Managing in a Time of Great Change*, Butterworth-Heinemann, 1995.

Drucker, Peter F., *The Pension Fund Revolution*, Transaction Publishers, New Brunswick, N.J., 1996.

Drucker, Peter F., *Managing for the Future: The 1990s and Beyond*, New York Truman Talley Books/Dutton, 1992.

Flannery, Timothy, *The Future Eaters*, Reed Books (Aust.), 1994.

Galbraith, John Kenneth, *A History of Economics*, Hamilton, 1987.

Gardiner, Wira, *Te Mura o te Ahi: The Story of the Maori Batallion*, Reed, 1992.

Gore, Al, *Earth in the Balance*, Houghton Mifflin, 1992.

Huntington, Samuel P., *The Clash of Civilizations and the Remaking of World Order*, Simon & Schuster, 1996.

Keynes, John Maynard, *Essays in Persuasion*, Hart-Davis, 1951.

Massie, Robert K., *Dreadnought: Britain, Germany and the Coming of the Great War*, Jonathan Cape, 1992.

Massie, Robert K., *Peter the Great: His Life and World*, Knopf, 1980.

Melbourne, Hineani, *Maori Sovereignty: The Maori Perspective*, Hodder Moa Beckett, 1995.

Moore, Mike, *On Balance*, MMSC Ltd, 1982.

Moore, Mike, *Pacific Parliament*, MMSC Ltd, 1983.

Moore, Mike, *The Added Value Economy*, Asia Pacific Economic News, 1984.

Moore, Mike, *Fighting for New Zealand*, MMSC Ltd, 1993.

Moore, Mike, *Children of the Poor*, Canterbury University Press, 1996.

Moynihan, D. Patrick, *On the Law of Nations*, Harvard University Press, 1990.

Moynihan, D. Patrick, *Pandaemonium*, Oxford University Press, 1993.

Naisbitt, John, *Megatrends: Ten New Directions for Transforming Our Lives*, Warner Books, 1984.

Naisbitt, John, and Aburdene, Patricia, *Megatrends 2000: Ten New Directions for the 1990's*, Morrow, 1990.

Olson, Mancur, *The Rise and Decline of Nations*, Yale University Press, 1984.

Orwell, George, *1984*, Secker & Warburg, 1949.

Oxley, Alan, *The Challenge of Free Trade*, Harvester Wheatsheaf, 1990.

Palmer, Geoffrey & Palmer, Matthew, *Bridled Power: New Zealand Government under MMP*, Oxford University Press, 1997.

Pfaff, William, *The Wrath of Nations*, Simon & Schuster, 1993.

Putnam, Robert, *Making Democracy Work*, Princeton University Press, 1993.

Reeves, Simon, *To Honour the Treaty: the Argument for Equal Seats*, Auckland Earth Restoration Ltd, 1995.

Ridley, Matt, *The Origins of Virtue*, Viking, 1996.

Schmidheiny, Stephan, in *New Zealand, A Nation That Can Work Again, The Proceedings of the Waipuna Seminar*, MMSC Ltd, 1993.

Shaw, Malcolm N., *International Law*, Cambridge University Press, 1997.

Simon, Julian Lincoln, *The State of Humanity*, Blackwell, 1996.

Singapore Government, *The Next Lap*, Times Editions, 1992.

Skidelsky, Robert, *John Maynard Keynes, a Biography*, London: Macmillan, 1983.

Smith, Adam, *The Theory of Moral Sentiments*, or *An Essay: A Dissertation on the Origin of Languages*, Wells and Lilly, 1817 (reprinted Regnery Pub., 1997).

Smith, Adam, *An Inquiry into the Nature and Causes of the Wealth of Nations*, 1776 (reprinted Methuen, 1950).

Stevens, Richard C., *The American Constitution and Its Provenance*, Rowman & Littlereld, 1997.

Toffler, Alvin, *Creating a New Civilization*, Turner Publishing Inc, 1994.

Toffler, Alvin, *Future Shock*, Pan, 1974.

Toffler, Alvin, *The Third Wave*, Morrow, 1980.

Vercoe, Andrew Eruera, *Educating Jake; Pathways to Empowerment*, Harper Collins, 1998.

Waterman, Robert H. Jr, *The Renewal Factor*, Bantam Books, 1987.

Wilson, James Q., *The Moral Sense*, Maxwell Macmillan International, 1993.

INDEX OF NAMES AND ORGANISATIONS